Written by Sally A Jones and Amanda C Jones
Illustrations by Annalisa Jones

Published by GUINEA PIG EDUCATION

2 Cobs Way,
New Haw,
Addlestone,
Surrey,
KT15 3AF.
www.guineapigeducation.co.uk

ISBN: 9781910824054

Dear kids,

If you are a fluent reader, you can work through this book and improve your reading comprehension. It will give you the skills that you will need later on for 11+ examinations and SATs.

Dear adults,

A collection of interesting articles to help your child practise essential reading comprehension skills. Each passage contains a series of questions, which requires the child to retrieve facts and explain information from texts.

Every passage contains vocabulary exercises, encouraging the child to search for words or phrases with the same meaning.

This book has been trialled by children of 6-9 years and has proved to be a valuable resource, that helps a child prepare for comprehensive papers later on e.g. for 11+ examinations.

Read the passage.

Read the questions

RETRIEVE

Answer the questions by finding (retrieving) facts and information from the text.

EXPLAIN

Answer the questions in a sentence, showing you can explain what you have read.

INFER   DEDUCE   INTERPRET

Write down your own ideas and opinions, saying what you think the writing means.

LANGUAGE

Say what words mean and why they have been used.

Comprehension is .....

Imagine a bird that has brilliant plumage and a long bill...

What else would you like to know about this animal?

Write down five questions.

Lets find out some information about the kingfisher.

The kingfisher is like a circus performer. He sits on a perch that is 15 metres above the water. He does a sudden dive, seizes a little fish in his long beak and flies back to his perch. Then, he swallows it headfirst.

All kingfishers are notable for their brilliant plumage and long bill, but they are unfriendly birds. If another bird comes near their fishing territory, they will chase it away. Kingfishers lay 5-8 eggs and their nest is made of a pile of fish bones

Many legends are connected to the European kingfisher. According to an old belief, the bird uses the seven days before the shortest day of the year to build a nest, which floats on water. They spend the next seven days laying eggs. People believed the sea was calm on these days.

Read the passage. Write the answers in a sentence.

1. How high is the kingfisher's perch?

   ....

   ....

2. What does the kingfisher eat?

   ....

   ....

3. How does it swallow its food?

   ....

   ....

4.

   a. What does the kingfisher look like?

   ....

   ....

   ....

   ....

   b. Why do you think it is so bright?

   ....

   ....

   ....

   ....

5. What are they like to the other birds? Why?

....

....

6. How many eggs do they lay?

....

....

7. In days gone by what did people believe about the kingfisher? Is this true do you think?

....

....

....

....

9. Can you think of another word or phrase that has the same meaning as these words in the passage?

performer   seizes   pile   legend   notable

....

actor   grabs   snatches   distinguished   tale

myth   heap   grasps   famous   fable

mound   showman   stack   renowned   artist

REMEMBER...

A capital letter begins a sentence.

A full stop ends a sentence.

A comma separates the items in a list.

Write out this passage correctly, putting in capital letters and full stops.

the kingfisher is like a circus performer he sits on a perch that is fifty feet above the water he does a sudden dive, seizes a little fish in his long beak and flies back to his perch then, he swallows it headfirst

all kingfishers are notable for their brilliant plumage and long bill, but they are unfriendly birds if another bird comes near their fishing territory, they will chase it away kingfishers lay 5-8 eggs and their nest is made of a pile of fish bones

Now write down what you can remember about the kingfisher.

Words to help you:

performer   seizes   brilliant   plumage   territory   connected

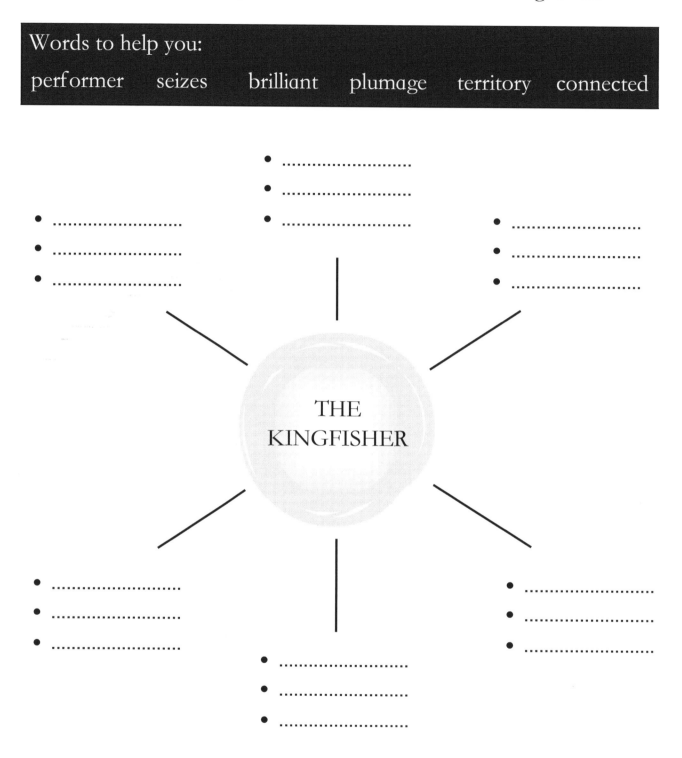

- ....
- ....
- ....

- ....
- ....

- ....
- ....
- ....

THE KINGFISHER

- ....
- ....

- ....
- ....
- ....

- ....
- ....
- ....

Think of another bird (parrot, toucan, swan, duck, black bird, blue tit). Write down as much information as you can about your chosen bird.

Use reference books or the internet to help you.

Imagine a time when huge beasts roamed the earth. They were called dinosaurs.

What else would you like to know about these creatures?

Write down five questions.

The word dinosaur comes from the Greek word 'deinos sauros', which means terrible lizard. In the Mesozoic age, there roamed many enormous creatures. They lived in swamps and jungles. They were strange looking creatures, like crocodiles and lizards today, but they were much bigger.

They had bulky bodies like elephants. They also had strong legs and a horny skin like an alligator. For example, the Brontosauras was as long as 600 feet.

How do we know such creatures existed? The answer is that fossilized castes of the remains have been found in the rocks. Scientists have been able to construct a fairly correct picture of what they looked like.

Read the passage. Write the answers in a sentence.

1. What does the word dinosaur mean?

   ....

   ....

2. When did they live?

   ....

   ....

3. In what places did they roam?

   ....

   ....

4. Describe some characteristics of dinosaurs.

   ....

   ....

   ....

   ....

5. The Brontosauras was .... feet long.

6. How do we know these creatures existed?

   ....

   ....

   ....

7. Why do you think dinosaurs no longer exist (became extinct?

....

....

....

....

....

8. Can you think of another word or phrase that has the same meaning as these words in the passage?

roamed	strange	bulky	construct
....	....	....	....
odd	wandered	curious	form
immense	walked	huge	prowled
build	establish	massive	extraordinary

Write out this passage correctly, putting in capital letters, full stops and one question mark.

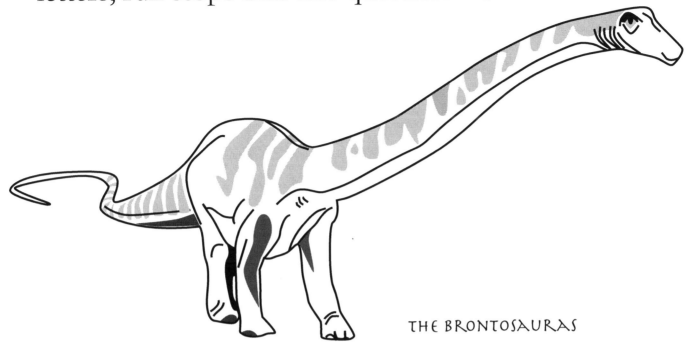

THE BRONTOSAURAS

the word dinosaur comes from the Greek word 'deinos sauros' in the mesozoic age, there roamed many enormous creatures they lived in the swamps and jungles they were strange looking creatures like crocodiles and lizards today, but they were much bigger

they had bulky bodies like elephants they also had strong legs and a horny skin like an alligator the brontosauras was as long as 600 feet

how do we know such creatures existed the answer is that fossilized castes of the remains have been found in the rocks scientists have been able to construct a fairly correct picture of what they looked like

Now write down what you can remember about dinosaurs.

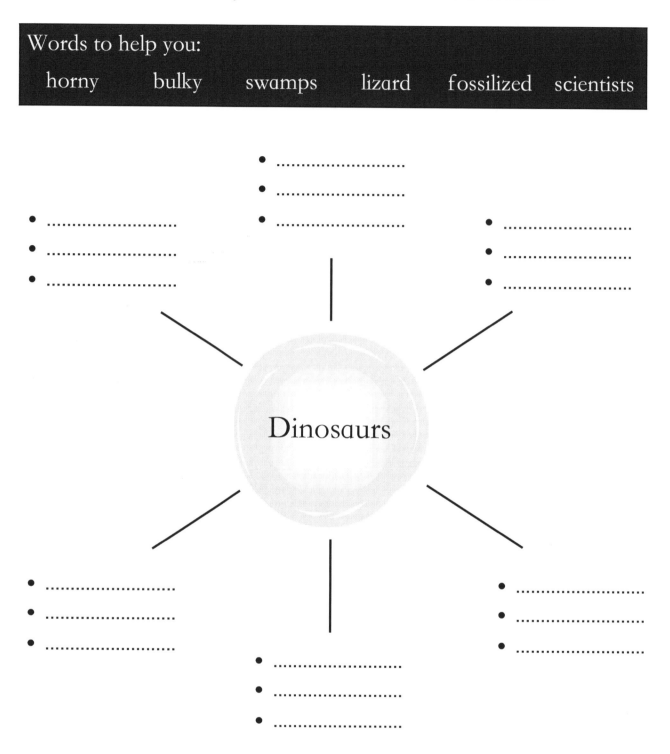

- ....
- ....
- ....
- ....
- ....
- ....
- ....
- ....

Dinosaurs

- ....
- ....
- ....
- ....
- ....
- ....
- ....
- ....
- ....

Think of another dinosaur (triceratops, tyrannosaurus rex, diplodocus, megalosaurus). Write down as much information as you can about your chosen dinosaur.

Use reference books or the internet to help you.

Dogs are man's best friend.

What else would you like to know about them?

Write down five questions about dogs.

MOUNTAIN DOGS FIND TRAVELLERS

Barry was a brave dog. He was trained by monks to rescue people, who were lost in the mountains.

One day a mountain climber fell over in a deep snowdrift. As he lay there, he heard the sound of a dog barking. Then, a big dog bounded up to him. The dog licked the man's face and hands, with his soft tongue, and let him drink from a flask round his neck.

After this, the dog took the man's cap and raced off. In a short time, he returned with a rescue party.

Some dogs had a paw in the war.

Some dogs were honoured as heroes. They were given medals because they were brave.

In the First World War, dogs went onto the battlefields. They helped feed the soldiers by carrying cans of soup. They bounded out into war zones, carrying first aid kits on their back.

DOG IN GAS MASK

A black and white setter, called Fred, dug out his master when he was buried by an explosion. There, he remained faithfully by his side, for 3 days and nights, until he was rescued.

Another dog, Michael, dragged his master, left for dead, back to the trenches and a sheepdog, called Felix, saved over one hundred lives.

Read the passage. Write the answers in a sentence.

1.   What was Barry trained to do?

....

....

....

2.   Who trained him?

....

....

....

3.   How did the dog help save the traveller's life? Find four ways.

....

....

....

....

4.   What is a hero?

....

....

....

....

....

....

5. Write down some of the ways dogs helped soldiers in the First World War.

....

....

....

....

6. Name two dogs that were heroes and write what they did.

....

....

....

7. Find another word or phrase that has the same meaning as these words in the passage.

brave	deep	bounded	honoured	faithfully
....	....	....	....	....

courageous	huge	pranced	devotedly	loyally
lovingly	fearless	massive	respected	recognised
leaped	regarded	heroic	great	padded

8. Why do you think dogs want to help their masters?

....

....

....

Write out this passage correctly, putting in capital letters, full stops and one apostrophe.

barry was a brave dog he was trained by monks to rescue people, who were lost in the mountains

one day a (traveller) mountain climber fell over in a deep snowdrift as he lay there, he heard the sound of a dog barking then, a big dog bounded up to him the dog licked the mans face and hands, with his soft tongue, and let him drink from a flask round his neck

after this, the dog took the man's cap and raced off in a short time, he returned with a rescue party

Now write down some facts about dogs. Write five
sentences about dogs. Here are some ideas to help you.

Dogs are pets;
dogs can work. They
are faithful friends.
They are loyal.

Dogs have: acute
hearing, keen eyes, sharp
teeth, strong legs, coarse
hair, a remarkable sense of
smell and strong
jaws.

Dogs pull
sledges in the Arctic. They
track criminals for the police.
They fetch and retrieve things.
They follow scents with their
noses. They follow a trail.

Dogs growl, howl
and bark. They
trample on things.
They bury bones.

Do you like dogs?

What do you like about them?

Think of a breed of dog (Labrador, Dalmatian, Poodle, Highland Terrier, Grey hound).

Write down as much information as you can about your chosen dog breed.

Use reference books or the internet to help you.

Grace Darling was a brave and fearless girl. She is famous today as a heroine.

What else would you like to know about her?

Write down five questions about her.

The true account of a brave girl.

FEARLESS GIRL RESCUES SURVIVORS

A fearless young girl, called Grace Darling (23), rowed out in a terrible gale last night, with her father, and rescued some survivors of a shipwreck.

The strong gales, in the North Sea, caused a paddle steamer to be ship wrecked on the rocks. When daylight came, the lighthouse keeper, who was Grace's father, saw survivors clinging to the rocks and in danger of being swept away by huge waves.

Grace urged her father to make a perilous trip out to the rocks, to rescue four men and one woman. Grace said that after they launched the boat, it was tossed around on the water like a cork in huge waves. When they got the people back to safety, Grace and her mother looked after them. Then, her father went back for the rest of the survivors.

Grace lived with her parents in a lighthouse on the Farne Islands, Northumberland. She was hailed a heroine and given a gold medal. As well as this, some money was raised to help her family.

Put Grace's story in order.

and she lived in a lighthouse on the Farne Islands.

and a steamer was wrecked on the rocks.

She was the daughter of a lighthouse keeper

Their small boat was tossed about on huge waves.

Grace Darling was born in Northumberland in 1915.

On the night of September 7th 1938, there was a terrible gale blowing in the North Sea

She pleaded with her father to row out to them. She took one of the oars.

Grace was awarded a gold medal

When day came, Grace saw survivors clinging to the rocks who were in terrible danger.

and some money was raised to help her family.

The fearless girl and her father managed to row out to the rocks and save the people.

Read the passage. Write the answers in a sentence.

1. Where did Grace live?

    ....

    ....

2. Why was Grace fearless?

    ....

    ....

3. What caused the paddle steamer to be wrecked?

    ....

    ....

4. What did Grace's father see on the rocks when daylight came?

    ....

    ....

5. How big were the waves?

    ....

6. What did Grace urge her father to do?

    ....

    ....

7. What was the sea like after the boat was launched?

   ....

   ....

8. How many survivors did they rescue?

   ....

   ....

9. What is a heroine?

   ....

   ....

   ....

10. What reward was Grace given?

    ....

11. Find another word or phrase that has the same meaning
    as these words in the passage.

    fearless   strong   clinging   huge   hailed

    ....

    daring   enormous   clasping   fierce

    acknowledged   powerful   brave   howling

    clutching   honoured   gigantic   courageous

Write out this passage correctly, putting in capital letters and full stops.

a fearless young girl, called grace darling (23), rowed out in a terrible gale last night, with her father, and rescued some survivors of a shipwreck

the strong gales, in the north sea, caused a paddle steamer to be ship wrecked on the rocks when daylight came, the lighthouse keeper, who was Grace's father, saw survivors clinging to the rocks and in danger of being swept away by huge waves

grace urged her father to make a perilous trip out to the rocks, to rescue four men and one woman grace said that after they launched the boat, it was tossed around on the water like a cork in huge waves when they got the people back to safety, Grace and her mother looked after them then, her father went back for the rest of the survivors grace lived with her parents in a lighthouse on the farne islands, northumberland she was hailed a heroine and given a gold medal as well as this, some money was raised to help her family

Now write down what you can remember about Grace Darling.

Words to help you:

fearless   rowed   gale   shipwrecked   survivors

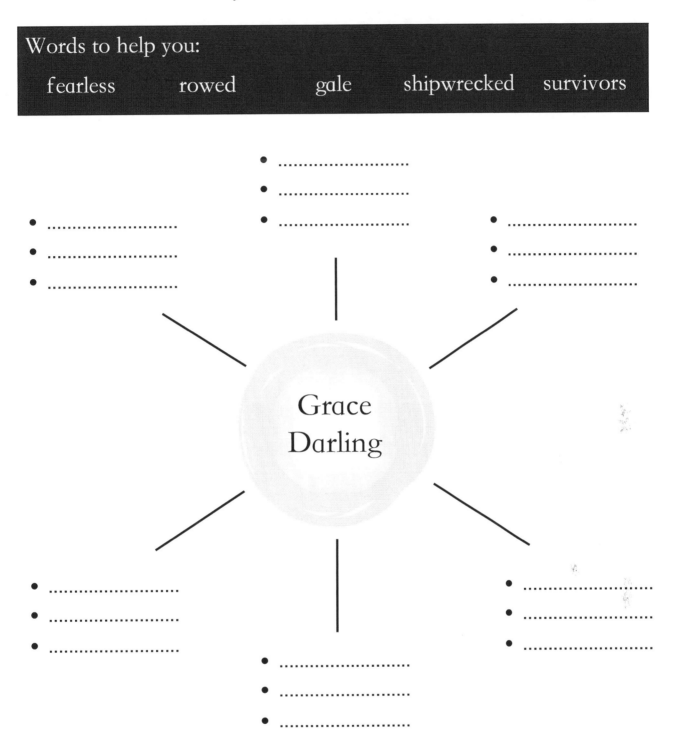

Grace
Darling

Think of another famous person (The Queen, Andy Murray, David Beckham). Write down as much information as you can about your chosen person.

Use reference books or the internet to help you.

Fuchsias are beautiful flowers

What would you like to know about them?

Write down five questions about fuchsias

It was the year of 1788. A man went to visit his friend. He was a sailor and lived down by the dock. As he entered the sailor's house, he was struck by some pretty flowers.

"What a beautiful plant," he exclaimed.

"Where did you get it?"

The sailor's wife smiled as she looked at the plant, which had come from far off Chile.

"My husband brought it from foreign parts," she answered proudly.

The man worked in a flower nursery. He recognised it as a rare plant. It was the same plant that had been brought back from South America, that same year and placed in Kew Gardens.

At once, he bought the plant from the woman. He took it back to his nursery and took some cuttings from it. From these cuttings, he had soon grown several hundred plants, which he sold for a high price.

From these and other specimens, bought from South America, Peru and Chile, we have gained these beautiful plants with brilliant, drooping and funnel shaped blossoms. They can be purple, rose and white and look pretty in our gardens.

Read the passage. Write the answers in a sentence.

1. In what year is this story told?

   ....

   ....

2. Who did the man visit?

   ....

   ....

3. Where did he live?

   ....

   ....

4. Why do you think he was surprised to see the plant?

   ....

   ....

5. Why was the wife proud of the plant do you think?

   ....

   ....

   ....

6. Which country had the plant come from?

   ....

   ....

7. Why did the nurseryman recognise it?

....

....

8. Why do you think he wanted to buy the plant from the wife?

....

....

9. Why did he sell the flowers he grew from his cutting for a high price?

....

....

10. Describe what the flowers look like.

....

....

11. Find another word or phrase that has the same meaning as these words in the passage.

entered	pretty	answered	proudly	rare
....	....	....	....	....

delicate	stated	unusual	joyfully
went into	scarce	replied	beautiful
explained	happily	attractive	accessed

Write out this passage correctly, putting in capital letters, full stops, one apostrophe, two sets of speech marks, one comma and a question mark.

it was the year of 1788 a man went to visit his friend he was a sailor and lived down by the docks as he entered the sailors house he was struck by some pretty flowers

what a beautiful plant he exclaimed where did you get it the sailor's wife smiled as she looked at the plant, which had come from far off Chile "my husband brought it from foreign parts," she answered proudly the man worked in a flower nursery he recognised it as a rare plant

Compare your work with the original.

Now write down what you can remember about fuchsias.

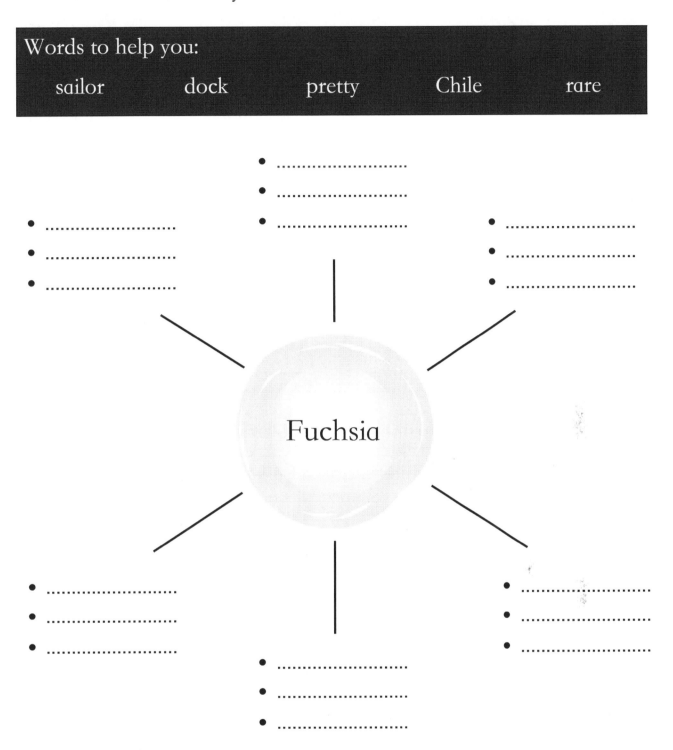

- ....
- ....
- ....

- ....
- ....
- ....

- ....
- ....
- ....

Fuchsia

- ....
- ....
- ....

- ....
- ....
- ....

Think of a type of flower (rose, tulip, sunflower, daffodil, orchid). Write down as much information as you can about your chosen flower.

Use reference books or the internet to help you.

Have you heard the incredible story about the man who befriended a lion?

ROAR...

What else would you like to know about this story?

Write down five questions you would like to ask.

Early one morning, in the first century AD, a weary man came to a cave in an African desert, flung himself on the ground and fell into a sound sleep.

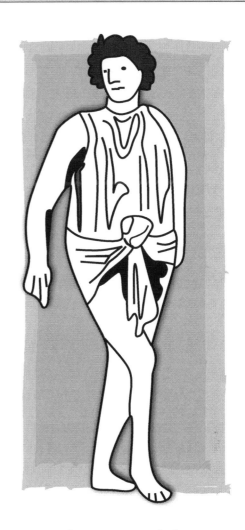

This poor man was a Roman slave named Androcles. He had been carried from Rome to North Africa, as a slave, by a cruel master. He had escaped from him in the dark.

Suddenly, Androcles was woken up by a terrible roar and he saw a huge lion standing in the entrance to the cave. He had fallen asleep in a lion's den. There was no way of escape. He waited for the lion to spring on him and tear him to pieces.

The lion did not move. It stood there moaning and licking one of its paws. Then, Androcles noticed that the lion's paw was pierced by a big thorn. Seeing the animal in pain, he forgot his fear and took hold of the paw to draw out the thorn. The story goes: he stayed with the lion for several years.

But then, Androcles longed to be with his fellow men. He left the lion, but he was caught by the Roman soldiers again and sent back to Rome. His punishment was to be thrown in a lion's cage, in a theatre, where crowds of people would watch.

Androcles was in the arena. He had only a lance to fight a hungry, ferocious lion. Androcles shook with fear as the cage was opened and the lion sprang out with a massive roar, but instead of rushing at him, it showed itself to be friendly and began to lick his hand. At that moment, he realised it was the very lion that had been his companion in the cave. He leaned against its mane and wept.

All the people watching were amazed. The emperor sent for Androcles, and when he heard his story, he set him free and gave him money. After this, wherever Androcles went the faithful lion followed him like a dog

Read the passage. Write the answers in a sentence.

1. When does this story take place?

    ....

2. What was the Roman slaves name?

    ....

3. What is a Roman slave?

    ....
    ....
    ....

4. Why did he escape do you think?

    ....
    ....
    ....
    ....

5. When he was in the cave, what woke him up?

    ....

6. What did he expect to happen to him?

    ....
    ....
    ....

7.   How do we know there is something wrong with the lion?

....

....

8.   Why did Androcles decide to help the lion?

....

....

....

....

9.   When he was caught, where did Androcles get sent and what was his punishment for escape?

....

....

....

....

....

10.   Describe what happened in the arena? Why were the audience shocked?

....

....

....

....

....

11. Find another word or phrase that has the same meaning as these words in the passage?

ferocious	weary	<u>sound</u> sleep
....	....	....
spring	moaning	pierced
....	....	....

leap   whining   uninterrupted   punctured   fatigued

exhausted   vicious   pounce   peaceful   stabbed

groaning   deep slumber   tired   wailing   cruel

12. How did Androcles and the lion feel about each other when they met up again?

....

....

....

....

....

13. What did the emperor do for Androcles when he heard the story?

....

....

....

....

Write out this passage correctly, putting in capital letters, full stops, one apostrophe and two commas (to separate a small clause in the middle paragraph).

early one morning, in the first century ad, a weary man came to a cave in an african desert, flung himself on the ground and fell into a sound sleep

this poor man was a roman slave named androdes he had been carried from rome to north africa as a slave by a cruel master he had escaped from him in the dark

suddenly, androdes was woken up by a terrible roar and he saw a huge lion standing in the entrance to the cave he had fallen asleep in a lions den there was no way of escape he waited for the lion to spring on him and tear him to pieces

Now write down what you can remember about this story.

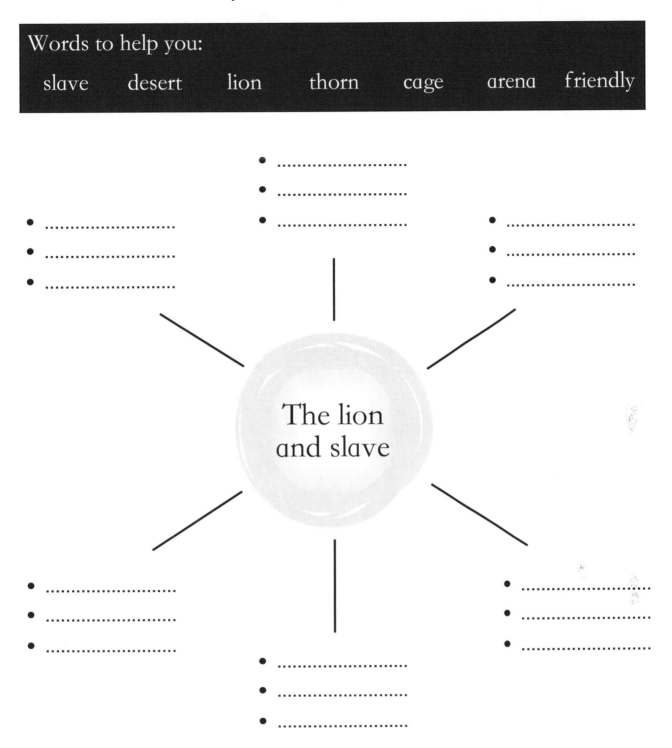

- ....
- ....
- ....

- ....
- ....

- ....
- ....
- ....

The lion
and slave

- ....
- ....
- ....

- ....
- ....
- ....

- ....
- ....
- ....

Can you think of another incredible story? Write down
as much information as you can about your chosen story.

Use reference books or the internet to help you.

Imagine an insect that has huge horns and sharp pincers.

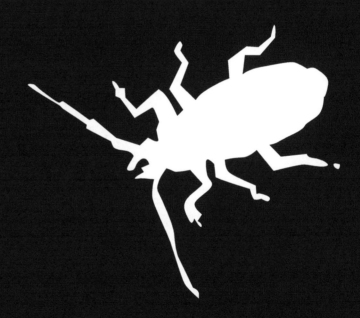

What else would you like to know about this insect?

Write down five questions about insects.

Let's find out some information on insects.

Some insects are masters of camouflage. They copy the colour and shape of a leaf so well, that their own brothers sometimes bite them by mistake thinking they are leaves.

Some insects imitate a stick of wood or the bark of a tree. They fool birds and men who look at them from a distance.

Insects use armour and weapons to protect themselves from enemies. If an ant could speak, he would say, "Feel my back. Do you see how tough, smooth and spongy it is? And the top of my head is covered with a tough horny substance called chitia."

Some beetles draw their heads and legs close and laugh at any small bird that tries to pierce their thick shell.

Some insects, like wasps and bees, can sting people.

Did you know that the common earwig frightens people, when he curls up with that terrible looking tail of his and with his snapping pincers? The truth: they couldn't hurt anything with their tails, but they are protected by the terror it causes.

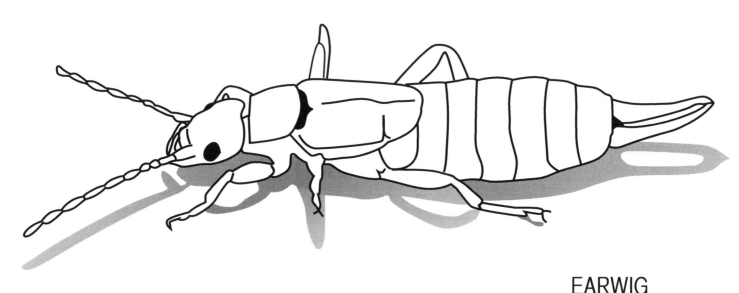

EARWIG

The stag beetle is so fierce with its huge horns that they scare insects and humans. However, if you dare to put your fingers towards his long pincers, he will not harm you because he can't pinch hard enough to do you any harm.

Read the passage. Write the answers in a sentence.

1. What does camouflage mean?

   ....

   ....

   ....

2. Write down some ways insects camouflage themselves?

   ....

   ....

   ....

3. What is an ants back like?

   ....

   ....

   ....

4. What is the substance on an ant's head called?

   ....

   ....

5. What is it made of? How does it protect him?

   ....

   ....

   ....

6. Name two insects that are not as terrifying as they look?

   ....

   ....

7. Name some insects that can be harmful to people.

   ....

   ....

   ....

   ....

8. Find another word or phase that has the same meaning as these words in the passage.

   copy   by mistake   fool

   ....

   pinch   scare

   ....

duplicate	trick	nip	accidentally
unintentionally	frighten	deceive	intimidate
mislead	emulate	squeeze	mirror

Write out this passage correctly, putting in capital letters and full stops.

some insects are masters of camouflage they copy the colour and shape of a leaf, so that their own brothers sometimes bite them by mistake thinking they are leaves

some insects imitate a stick of wood or the bark of a tree they fool birds and men who look at them from a distance

Write out this passage putting in capital letters, full stops, a question mark, commas and speech marks where needed.

insects use armour and weapons to protect themselves from enemies if an ant could speak he would say
Feel my back. Do you see how tough smooth and spongy it is And the top of my head is covered with a tough horny substance called chitia

the stag beetle is so fierce with its huge spiky and fearsome horns they scare insects and humans. However if you dare to put your fingers towards his long shiny pincers, he will not harm you he can't pinch hard enough to do you any harm.

Now write down what you can remember about insects.

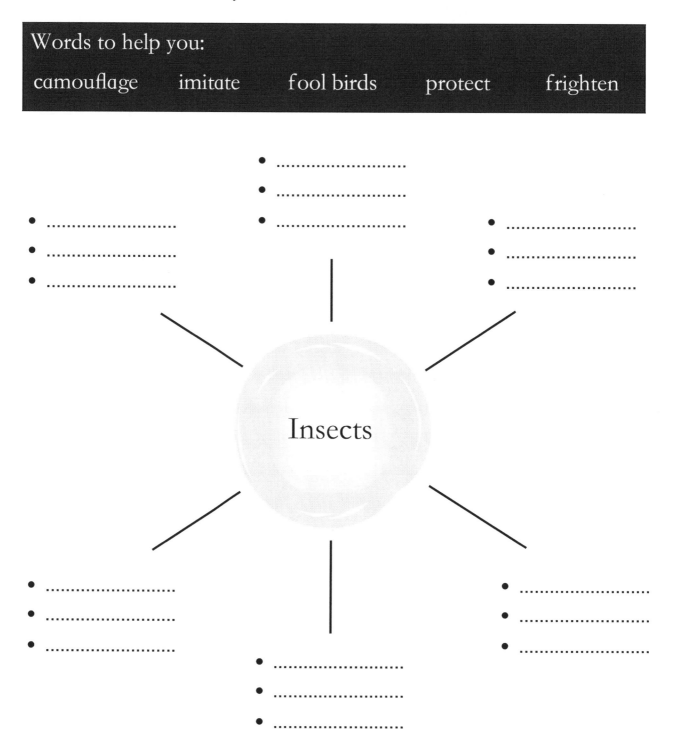

- ....
- ....
- ....

- ....
- ....

- ....
- ....
- ....

Insects

- ....
- ....
- ....

- ....
- ....
- ....

- ....
- ....
- ....

Think of an insect (green fly, ladybird, stick insect). Write down as much information as you can about your chosen insect.

Use reference books or the internet to help you.

"Tell me a story great grandad about the days long ago when you were young."

"Well, if you promise to be good, I might have a tale to tell."

Long ago, there was a baby elephant
called Mogul. He lived in the jungle with
his herd. He was the cutest little elephant
with pink and white patches on one eye
and a little trunk. He liked to play hide
and seek with the other elephants, but at
the first sign of danger, he would cuddle
up between his mother's legs as she
shuffled along.

One terrible night, the elephants heard some strange noises and sensed danger. Some hunters had come and were trapping the elephants, driving them into an enclosure and tying them up so they could train them to work. Mogul's mother was terrified. She ran far away and the hunters saw a funny, little calf charging up and down. They chased him, but he ran very fast, with his trunk in the air. "Come here little one," the men called, but Mogul flapped his big ears and he shrieked loudly. He was very angry.

In a few minutes, the men had tied him to a tree in the enclosure. The baby elephant shrieked at the top of his voice, but the hunters were not unkind men. They saw that he was too young to eat with the other elephants they had trapped, and they found he couldn't suck milk from a bowl up the long tubes in his trunk, so they brought him a bottle instead. He sucked greedily from it.

Read the passage. Write the answers in a sentence.

1. The baby elephant lived in ....

2. He was cute because he had ....

3. He liked to play .... but if he sensed danger he would ....

4. One terrible night the elephants heard ....

5. The hunters were ....

6. Mogul's mother was .... and she ....

7. When the hunters found Mogul he was .... and ....

8.   When they chased him he ....

.... and ....

.... and ....

9.   After they secured him to the tree Mogul ....

....

10.   The men found he was too young to eat elephant

food because ....

and ....

11.   After this they bought him a ....

....

12.   Find another word or phase that has the same meaning
as these words in the passage.

cutest	shuffled	sensed	trapping
....	....	....	....
charging	flapped	shrieked	tied
....	....	....	....

discerned   dragged   ensnaring   sweetest   storming

capturing   stampeding   squealed   shook   felt

scuffled   chained   appealing   imprisoning   scraped

Write out this passage correctly, putting in capital letters, full stops and commas, to separate the clauses in the long sentences.

long ago, there was a baby elephant called mogul he lived in the jungle with his herd he was the cutest little elephant with pink and white patches on one eye and a little trunk he liked to play hide and seek with the other elephants, but at the first sign of danger he would cuddle up between his mother's legs as she shuffled along

Mogul was now one year old and his new master built him a shed by the stables. Every day, the little elephant would trot to the kitchen to receive his bottle of milk and some bananas. He was as friendly as a dog. In the morning, he would trot up to his master, twist his little trunk round his arm and beg to be taken to the fruit trees. The servants let him carry fodder on his back for the other elephants.

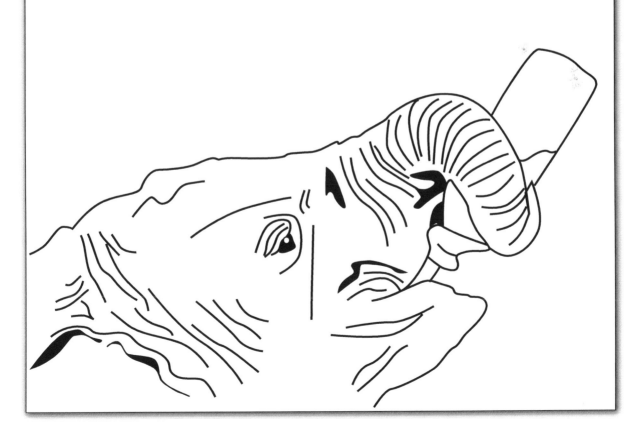

One morning, Mogul stepped out of his shed, into the bright sunshine, and trotted towards the house to fetch his breakfast. He gulped down the creamy, white milk in his bottle, and ate a bunch of bananas, and as he returned to his shed, he passed the window. There, he spied some delicious oranges, piled up in a china bowl. "Delicious!" he thought.

Later, Mogul saw his master leave the house on his way to work. He was playing in the garden, but he was bored, so he lumbered around to the back door, remembering the oranges on the table. Mogul pushed on the door and it opened. He stared in to the dark room. The oranges were still there, so he curled his trunk round a juicy orange, raised his trunk and placed the orange in his mouth greedily. He ate another and another, until half of them were gone. Mogul was enjoying the feast. He swung his trunk from side to side as he chewed, but his trunk hit the beautiful china bowl and it hit the floor, splintering into a thousand pieces and scattering the rest of the fruit. Oh no! What should he do?

At that moment, the door opened and his master returned.

"What are you doing inside, you naughty creature?" he gasped. "Look at all this mess! You have broken my best china bowl. GET OUT OF HERE." Mogul lumbered round the room trying to find the door, as the master pulled and pushed him, but he only sent more things flying. Mogul did not want the master to be cross, so he put his trunk round his arm and coaxed him to be taken to the fruit fields.

Read the passage. Write the answers in a sentence.

1. When Mogul was one year old he ate ....

....

2. At night he slept in a ....

....

3. Mogul was as friendly as a ....

.... because ....

....

4. Tell the story of how Mogul took fruit from the basket of oranges.

....

....

....

....

....

....

....

....

....

....

....

....

The time came for Mogul, the baby
elephant, to be trained for work. He was
fitted with a rope harness and taught to
pull or push at a single command. On his
back, he had a driver, who guided him
by drumming with his heels and
touching his ears with a hook. Mogul
became fond of him because he talked to
the baby elephant, calling out 'ho'.

When Mogul became older and his tusks had grown, he was given the task of piling teak logs in the timber yard. He would curl his trunk over the logs, rise up and carry them to the proper pile, where he placed them on top. One day, Mogul was carrying stones. Suddenly, one of the stones fell. It slipped part way down the cliff. His driver gave the order, "Get it," but Mogul refused to budge, because he sensed danger. "No, no, no," he shrieked.

After this, the men saw the edge of the cliff was about to crumble, so they let down a chain over the stone and Mogul pulled and pulled until it came up. They knew Mogul had grown wise, as well as a strong and faithful elephant. In fact, he was the best young elephant in the whole of India.

Read the passage. Write the answers in a sentence.

1. When Mogul was trained, he was fitted
with ....

2. His driver sat on .... who
....

3. When his tusks had grown, Mogul worked ....
....

4. His job was to ....
....
....

5. When the stone fell over the cliff, Mogul ....
.... because ....
....

6. The men put a .... over the
stone so ....

7. They realised Mogul was .... as well
as ....
....

8. Find another word or phase that has the same meaning as these words in the passage.

trained	fond	budge	guided
....	....	....	....

piling	crumble	pulled and pulled	sensed
....	....	....	....

collapse	devoted	supervise	heaved	shift
instructed	hauled	move	lugged	liked
perceived	break up	stacking	directed	taught

Write out this passage correctly, putting in capital letters, full stops, commas and speech.

suddenly one of the stones fell it slipped part way down the cliff his driver gave the order get it but Mogul refused to budge because he sensed danger no, no, no he shrieked

after this the men saw the edge of the cliff was about to crumble so they let down a chain over the stone and mogul pulled and pulled until it came up they knew Mogul had grown wise as well as a strong and faithful elephant in fact he was the best young elephant in the whole of India

Practise some more punctuation.

come here little one the men called

in the morning he would trot up to his master twist his little trunk round his arm and beg to be taken to the fruit trees

delicious he thought

he was playing in the garden but he was bored so he lumbered around to the back door

the oranges were still there so he curled his trunk around a juicy orange

what are you doing inside you naughty creature he gasped

the little elephant slipped into the house helped himself to a basket of oranges and swept some china onto the floor

Now write down what you can remember about Mogul.

Words to help you:

jungle	herd	shuffle	trained	stout tusk
harness	curl	rise		

- ....
- ....

- ....
- ....

- ....
- ....

MOGUL

- ....
- ....

- ....
- ....

- ....
- ....

Write five sentences about elephants.

....

....

....

....

....

Get over this message early on.

Stories and books are **GREAT**...

AMAZING!

It is **FUN** to read.

Later on so many children stop reading and prefer computer games or watching TV. Here are some ways we can help:

- Parents: sit with your child and read the pages from your child's school reading book, working out new words using phonics.

- Encourage children to choose books from the library or book club to read or to have read aloud.

Some children need to be encouraged. We can help them build up confidence in reading and writing skills.

- Parents: read bedtime stories with your child.

- Get your child to recount stories they have heard on TV, DVD, films and at story time.

Parents: when you read a story, talk about it with your child. Ask your child, if they know:

- Who is in it?
- Where they are?
- What is happening?
- What they think will happen next?
- How they expect the story to end?
- What they liked best or why it happened?

Encourage you child not to give you one-word answers, but to use lots of detail when they talk about what is happening in the story.

Encourage them:

- To explain clearly why they think something is happening in a story.

- To give reasons as to what they think it means for the characters.

IMPORTANT

Yes even at this stage!

Encourage your child to think beneath the surface, to form his or her own opinions.

Your child will read every day:

- in shops, along streets
- on posters and notices
- on T.V., on invitations
- on instructions, ingredients

and so on....

When you are out and about, ask your child questions. Can you read the sign? What does it mean?

Answers

Remember that the child should write their answers in sentences.

Page 6

1. 50 ft above water
2. fish
3. headfirst
4 a. brilliant plumage and a long bill
4 b.
- to be seen
- to stand out
- to appear aggressive
- to frighten other birds away
5. unfriendly. They chase them away.
6. 5-8 eggs
7. Kingfishers use the seven days before the shortest day of the year to build a nest, which floats on water. There may be some truth, as legends are passed down from generation to generation.
8.
performer – showman, artist, actor
seizes – snatches, grabs, grasps
pile – heap, stack, mound
legend – myth, tale, fable
notable – renowned, distinguished, famous

Page 9

The kingfisher is like a circus performer. He sits on a perch that is fifty feet above the water. He does a sudden dive, seizes a little fish in his long beak and then flies back to his perch. Then he swallows it headfirst.

All kingfishers are notable for their brilliant plumage and long bill, but they are unfriendly birds. If another bird comes near their fishing territory, they will chase it away. Kingfishers lay 5-8 eggs and their nest is made of a pile of fish bones.

Page 13

1. It comes from the Greek word 'deinos sauros', meaning terrible lizard.
2. Mesozaic age
3. swamps and jungles
4. They have bulky bodies like elephants. They also have strong legs and a horny skin like an alligator.
5. 600 feet long
6. Fossilized castes of their remains have been found in rocks.
7.
- caught a disease
- ran out of food
- bad weather like an Ice Age destroyed them or a meteorite, from space, crashed into earth.
8.
roamed – wandered, walked, prowled
strange – odd, curious, extraordinary
bulky – immense, massive, huge
construct – form, build, establish

Page 15

The word dinosaur comes from the Greek word 'deinos sauros'. In the Mesozoic age there roamed many enormous creatures. They lived in the swamps and jungles. They were strange looking creatures like crocodiles and lizards today, but they were much bigger.

They had bulky bodies like elephants. They also had strong legs and a horny skin like an alligator. The brontosauras was as long as 600 feet.

How do we know such creatures existed? The answer is that fossilized castes of the remains have been found in the rocks. Scientists have been able to construct a fairly correct picture of what they looked like.

Page 20

1. rescue people lost in the mountains
2. monks
3.
- licked him
- let him drink from a flask
- took his cap
- returned with rescuers
4. someone who does a brave deed
5.
- helped to feed soldiers
- carried cans of soup
- carried first aid kits on their backs
6.
- Fred dug his master out when he was buried by an explosion and waited faithfully by his master for three days, until he was rescued
- Michael dragged his injured master back to the trenches, where he could be helped
7.
- brave – courageous, fearless, heroic
- deep – huge, great, massive
- bounded – pranced, leaped, padded
- honoured – respected, recognised, regarded
- faithfully – loyally, devotedly, lovingly
8. they are loyal, faithful and devoted to people who look after them

Page 22

Barry was a brave dog. He was trained by monks to rescue people who were lost in the mountains.

One day a (traveller) mountain climber fell over in a deep snowdrift. As he lay there, he heard the sound of a dog barking. Then a big dog bounded up to him. The dog licked the man's face and hands with his soft tongue and let him drink from a flask round his neck.

After this, the dog took the man's cap and raced off. In a short time he returned with a rescue party.

Page 27

- Grace Darling was born in Northumberland in 1915.
- She was the daughter of a lighthouse keeper
- and she lived in a lighthouse on the Farne Islands.
- On the night of September 7th 1938, there was a terrible gale blowing in the North Sea
- and a steamer was wrecked on the rocks.
- When day came, Grace saw survivors clinging to the rocks, who were in terrible danger.
- She pleaded with her father to row out to them. She took one of the oars.
- Their small boat was tossed about on huge waves.
- The fearless girl and her father managed to row out to the rocks to save people.
- Grace was awarded a gold medal
- and some money was raised to help her family.

Page 28

1. Farne Islands Northumberland, with her parents
2. She was prepared to risk her life and row out in a terrible gale.

Tablature Notation

Standard Notation

Lágrima

Tango

Francisco Tárrega

Fine

6

D. S. al Fine

7

Tango Español

Isaac Albeniz

9

10

Danza Española No. 5

E. Granados

11

12

13

Tango No. 2

Agustín Barrios Mangoré

14

16

17

Don Pérez Freire

Tango

Agustín Barrios Mangoré

18

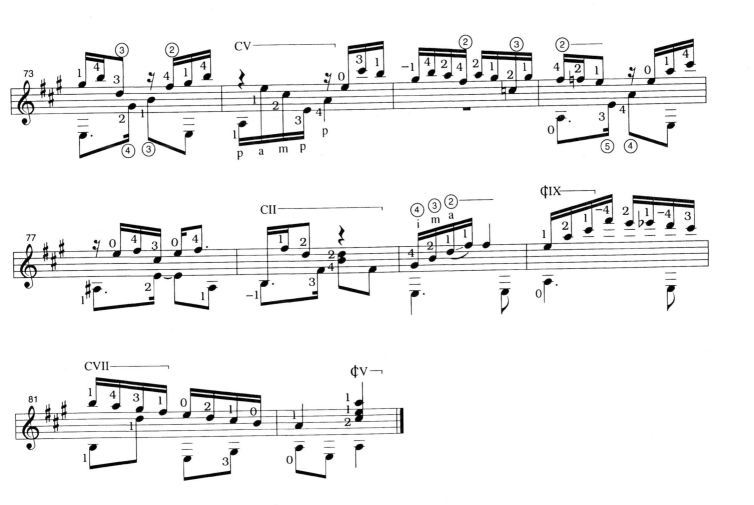

¡Ayer se la llevaron!

Tango Canción

Daniel Fortea

23

24

Musa Argentina

Celebre Tango Argentino

Espiga - Fortea

Tango

La Paloma

S. Yradier
F. Tárrega

'O sole mio

Tango

E. di Capua
Transcription by F. Tárrega

Del Ferrol a La Habana

Collection of Tangos for Guitar

J. Parga

34

This page has been left blank
to avoid awkward page turns.

(Del Ferrol a La Habana)

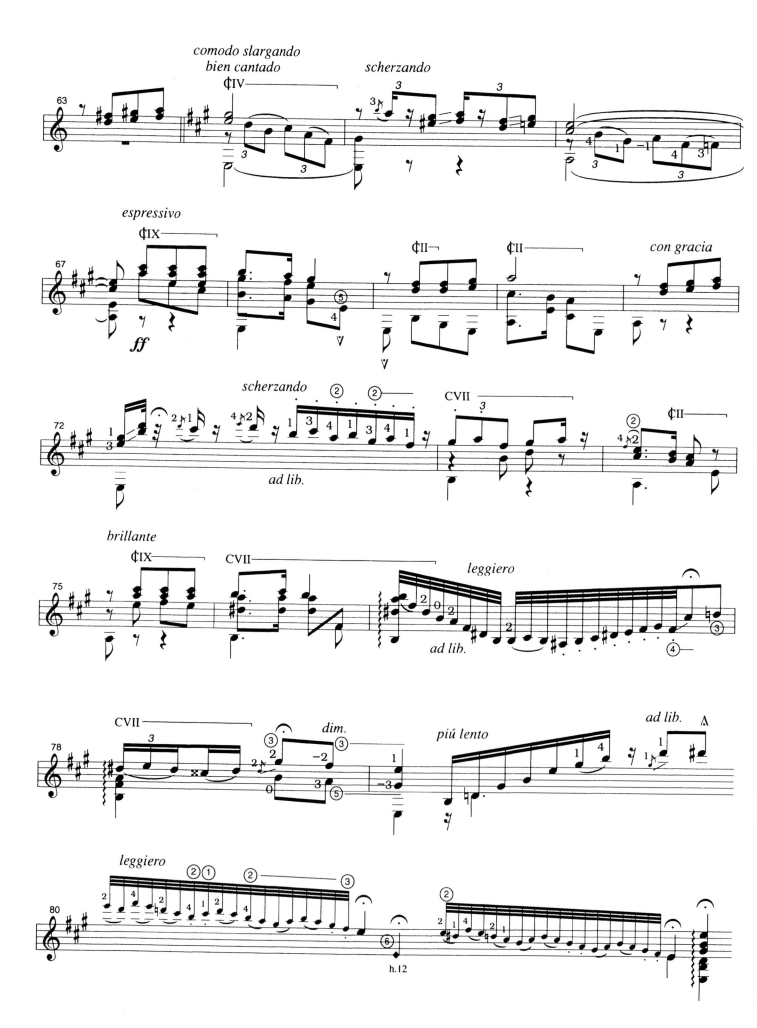

(proceed to No. 2)

(Del Ferrol a La Habana)

(proceed to No. 3)

(Del Ferrol a La Habana)

(proceed to No. 4)

43

(Del Ferrol a La Habana)

No. 5   Danza Cubana

This page has been left blank
to avoid awkward page turns.

A ti solita!...

For Two Guitars   Habanera   F. P. Spreafico

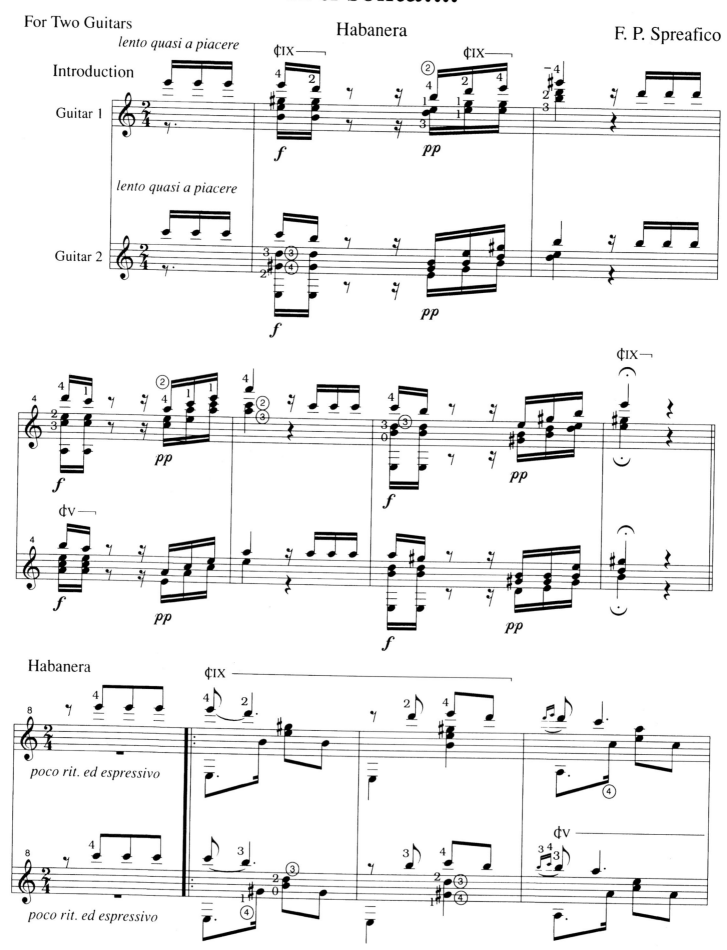

49

50

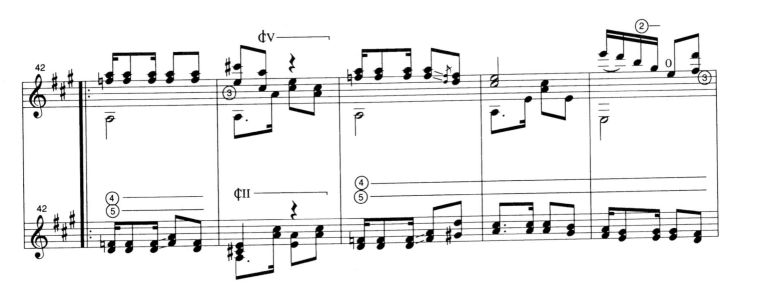

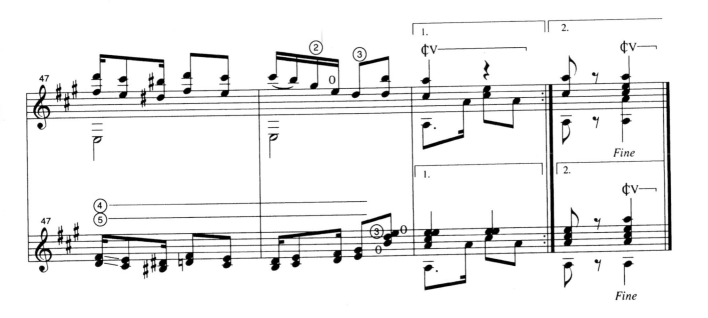

Clarita

Tango, Opus 3

Julian Ortiz

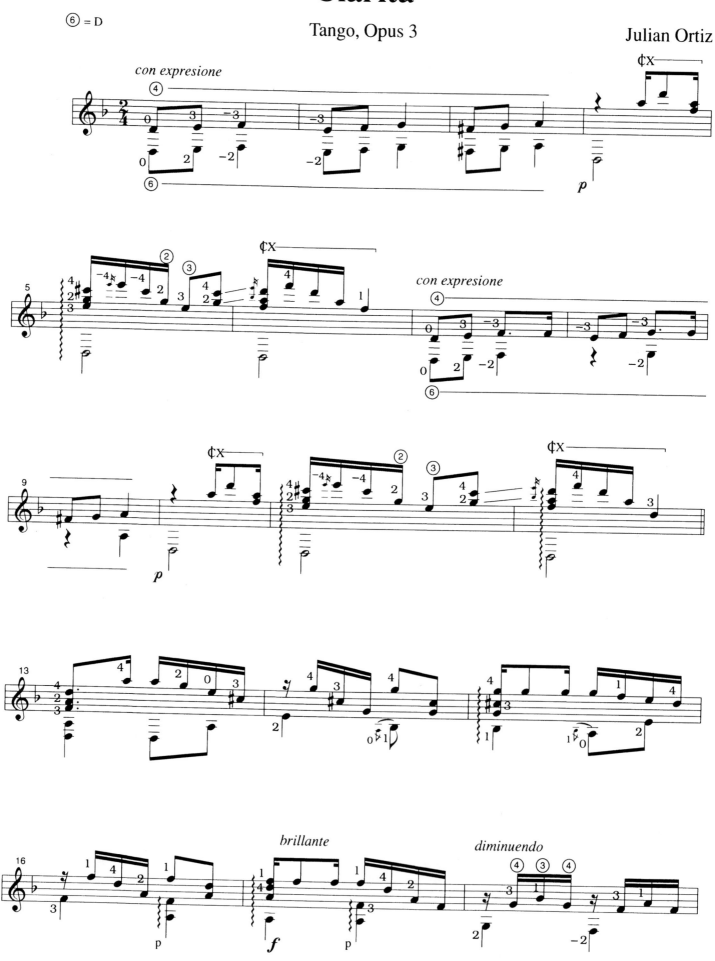

Anhelando

Tango de Salon

Julian Ortiz

bien marcado con expresion

Junta al Farol

Tango Criollo

Vincente Caprino M.

This page has been left blank
to avoid awkward page turns.

Don Martín

Tango Criollo

Vincente Caprino M.

58

D. Juan Carlos

Tango Criollo

Vincente Caprino M.

61

62

Romero

Tango

A. Galluzo

El Alero

Tango Pajuerano

Juan Maglio

Tablature Notation

Lágrima

Tango

Francisco Tárrega

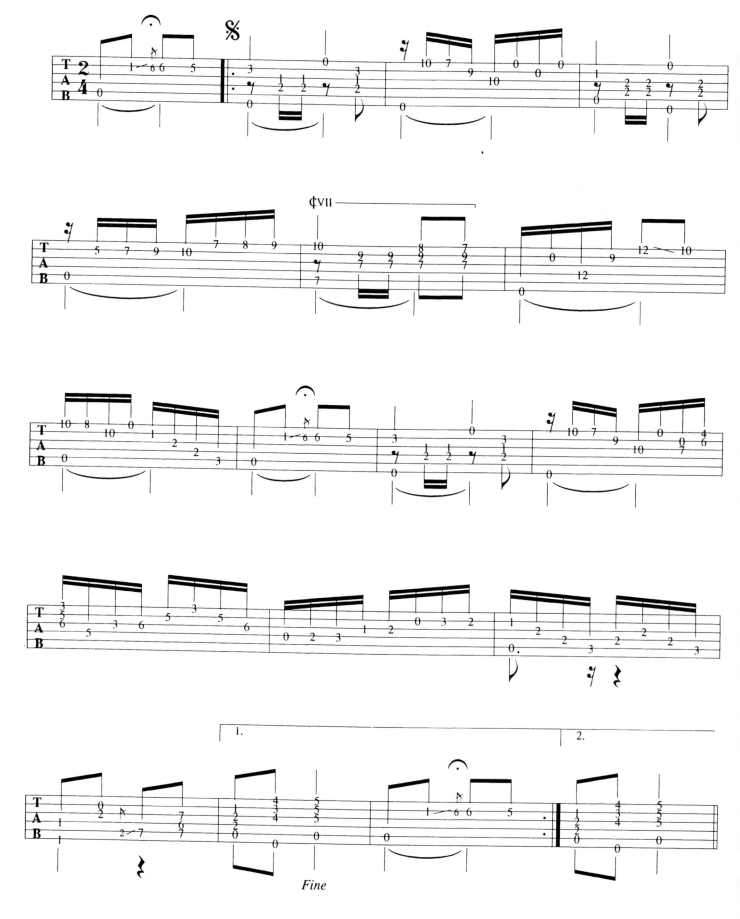

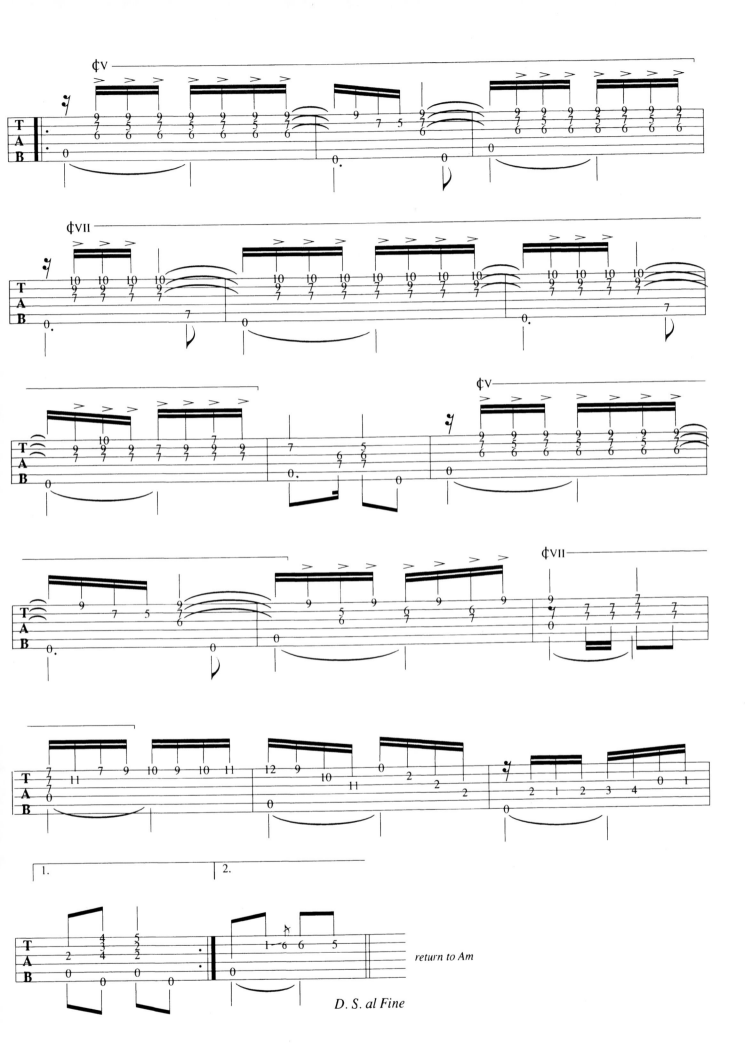

return to Am

D. S. al Fine

Tango Español

Allegretto

Isaac Alneniz

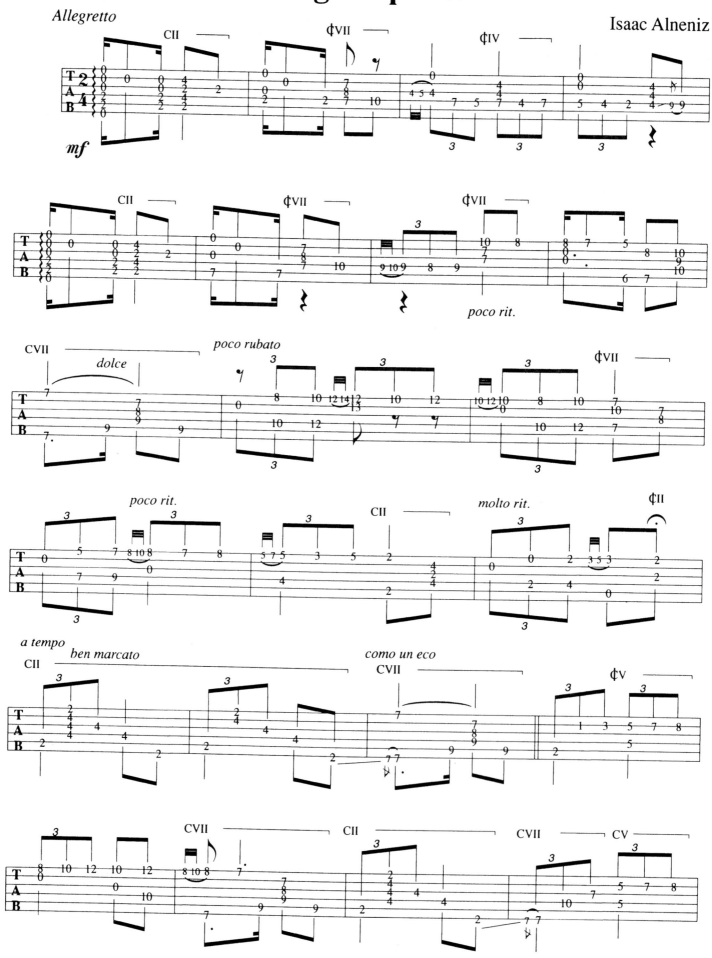

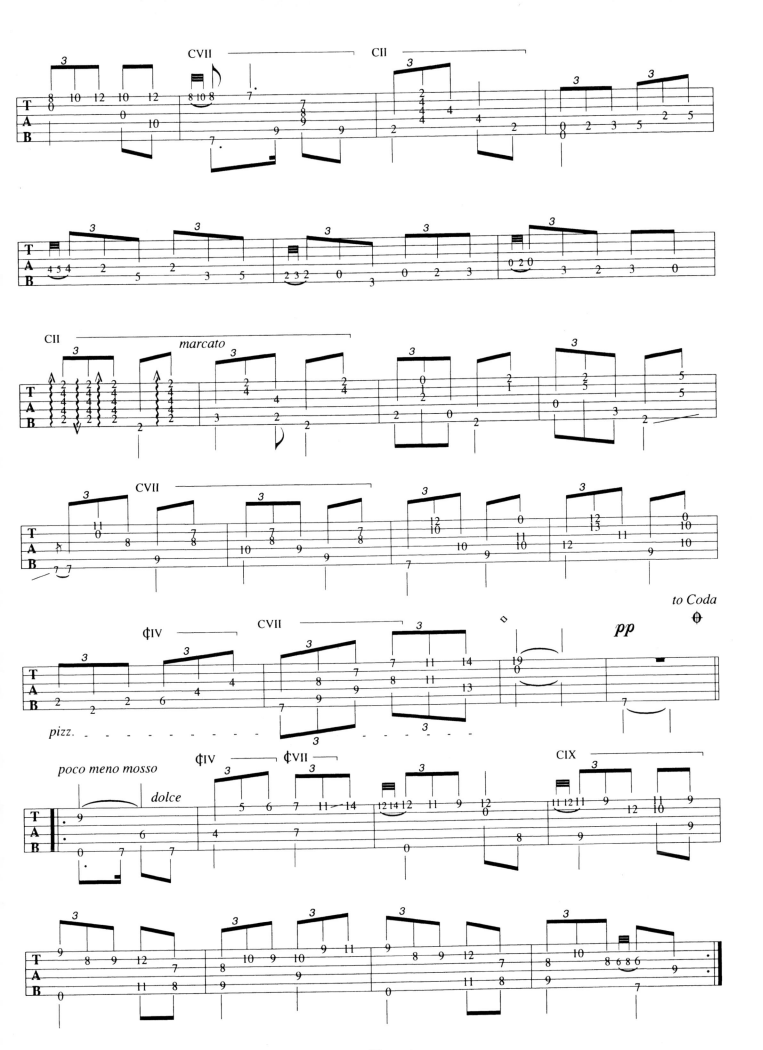

71

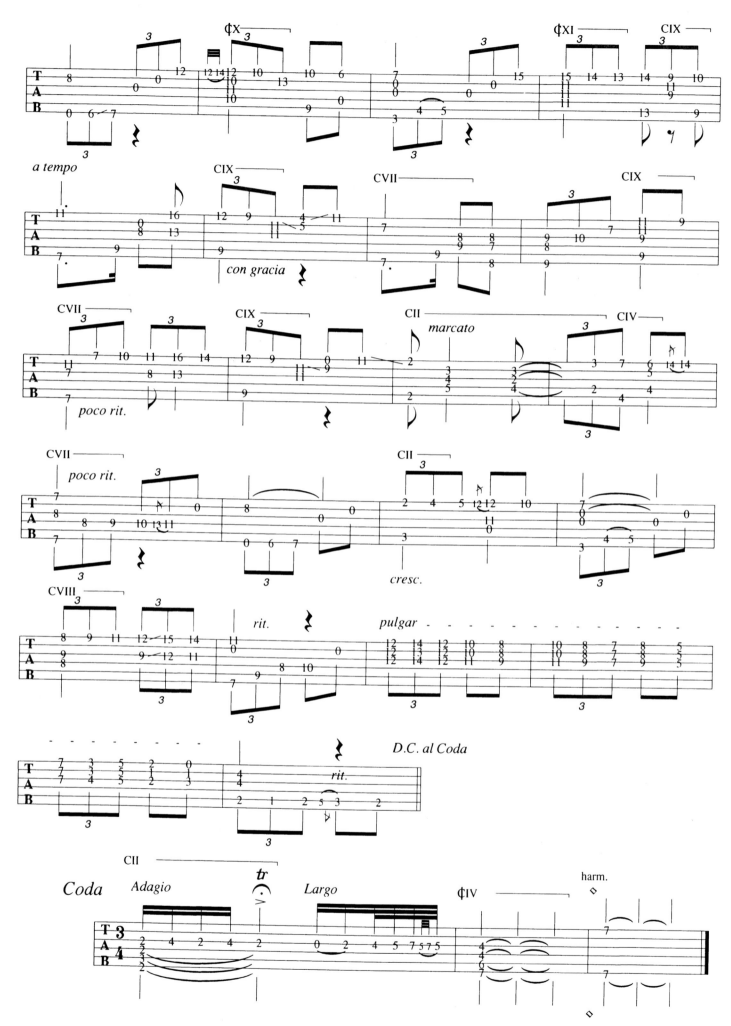

Danza Española No. 5

E. Granados

Andante Allegro

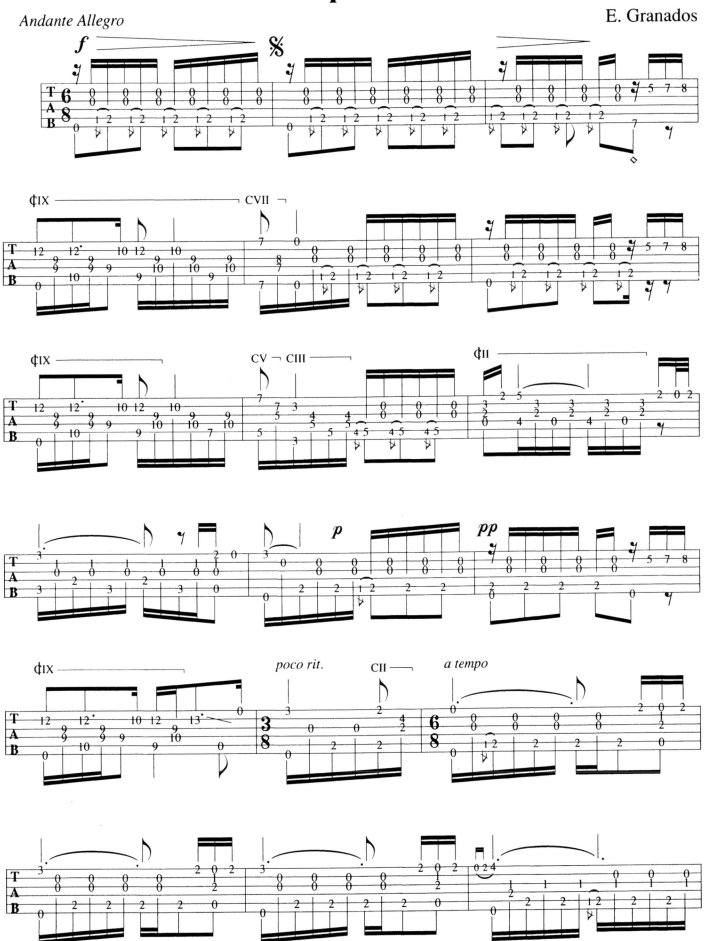

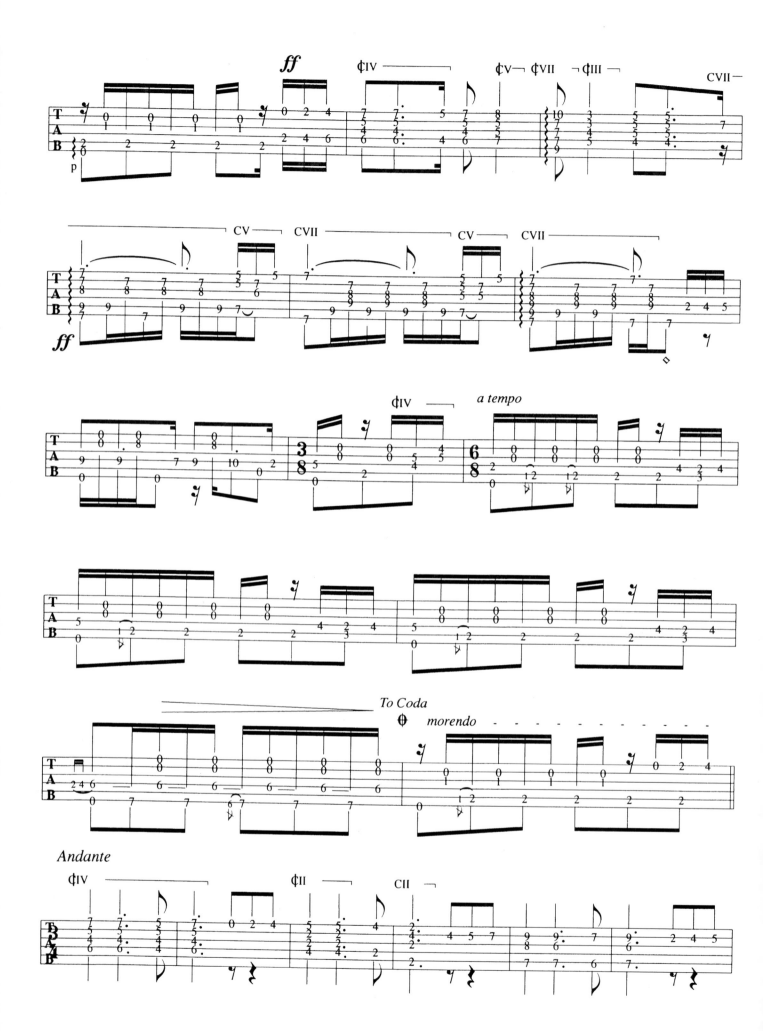

74

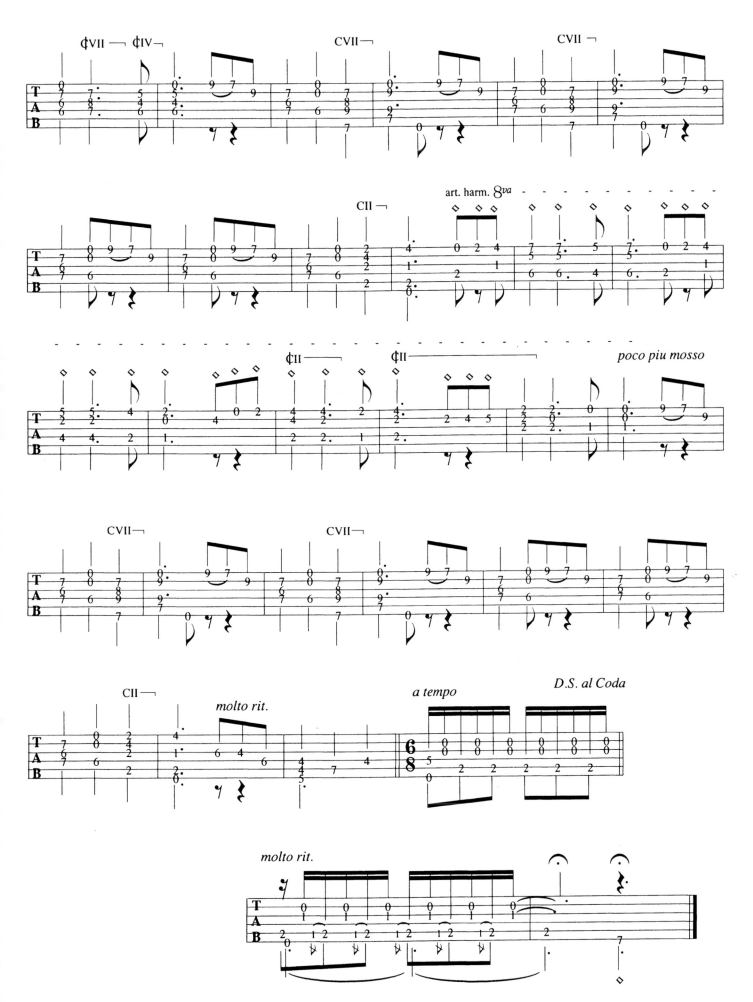

Tango No. 2

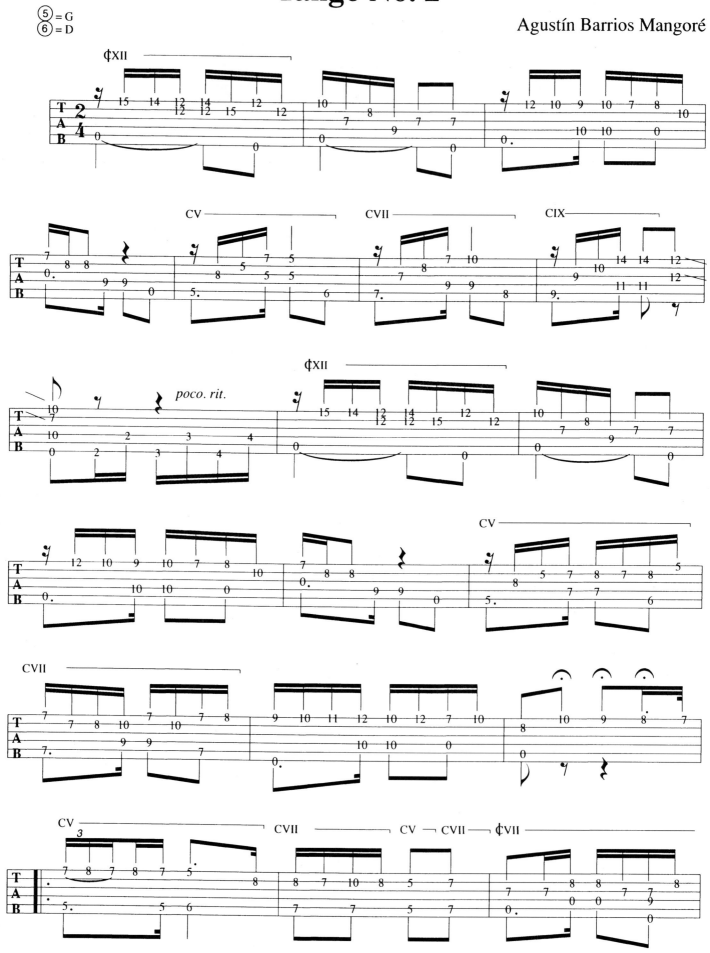

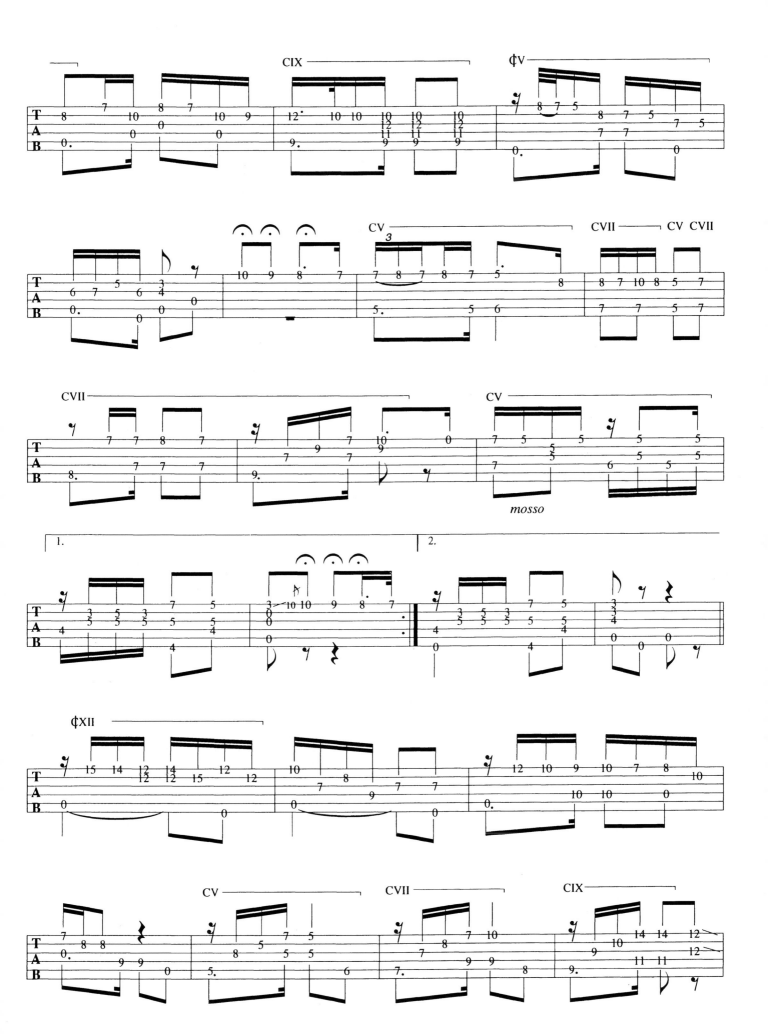

77

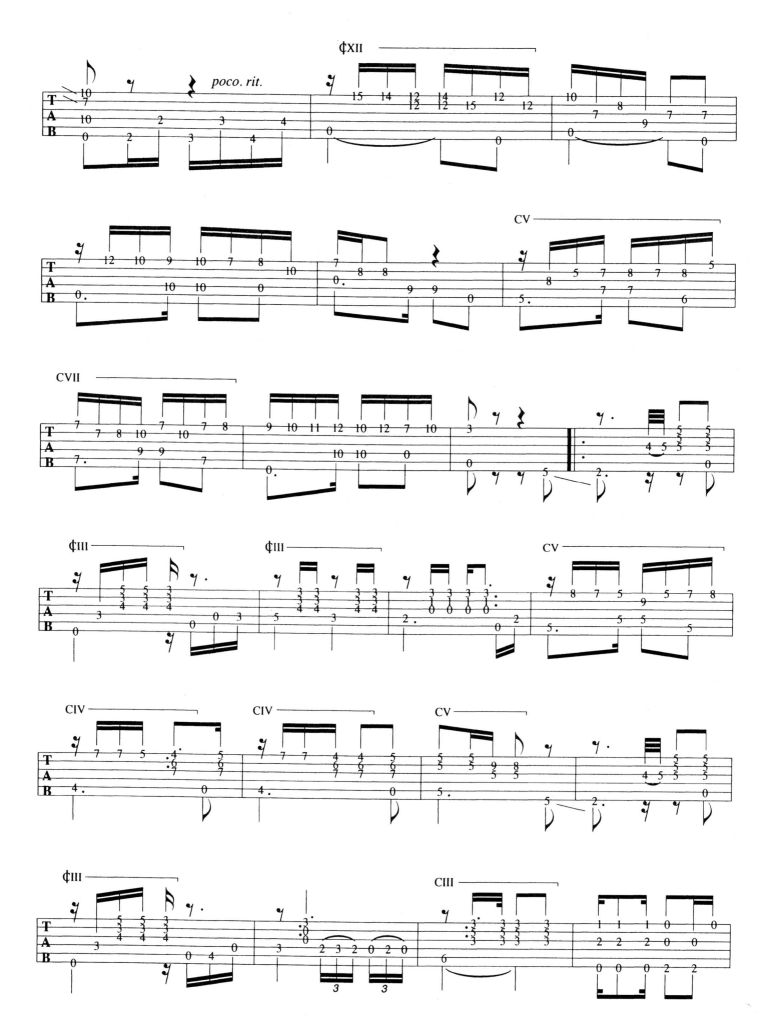

79

Don Pérez Freire

Tango   Agustín Barrios Mangoré

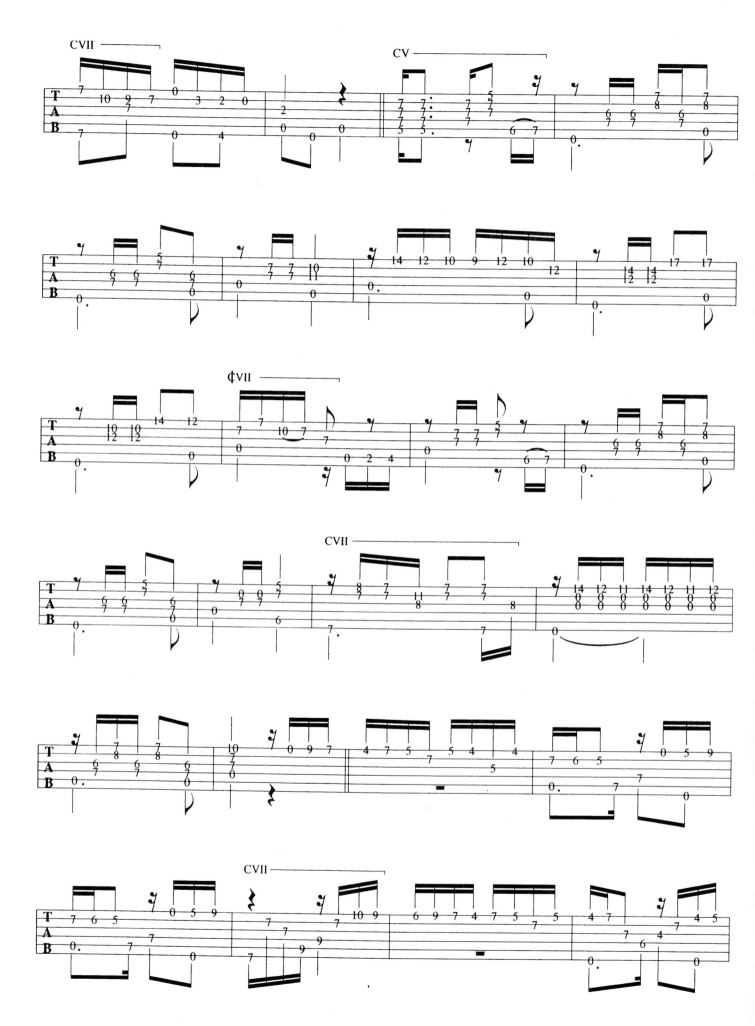

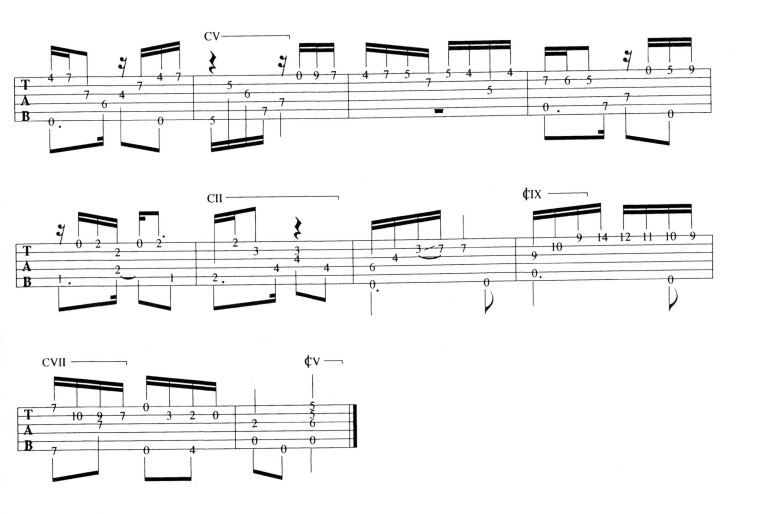

¡Ayer se la llevaron!

Tango Canción

Daniel Fortea

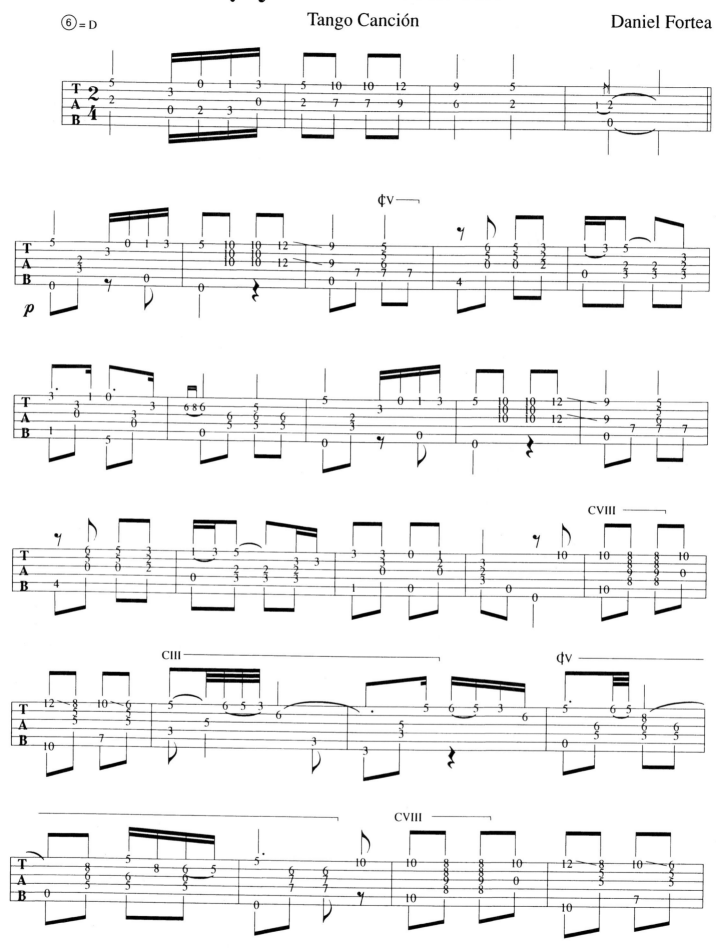

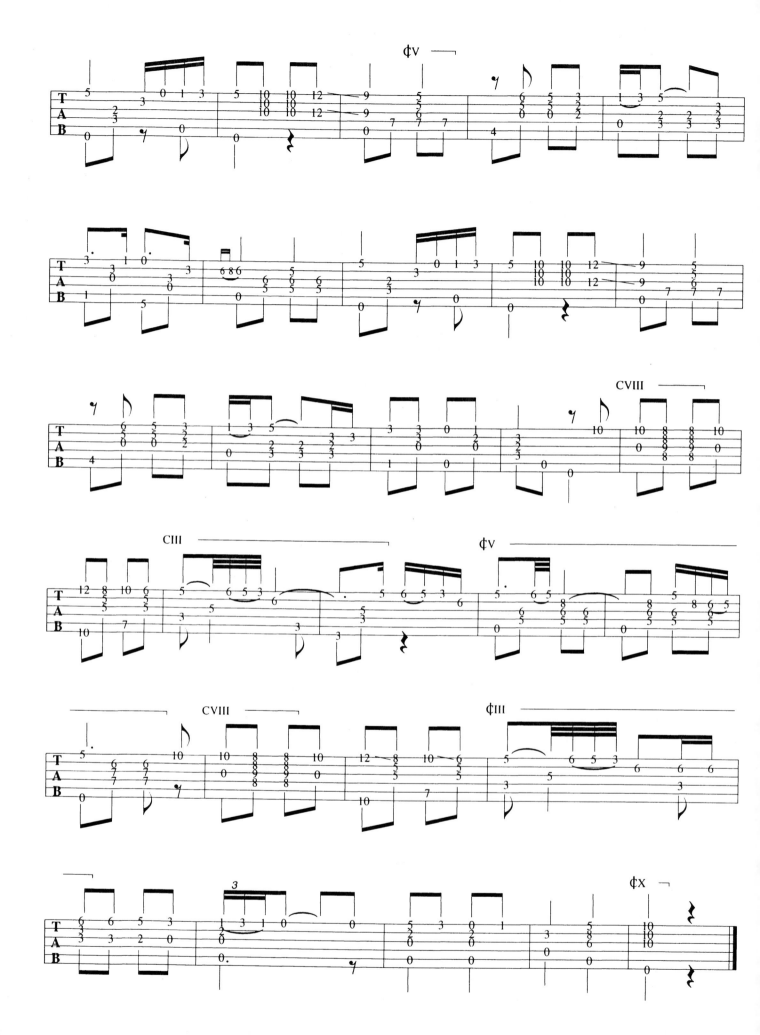

Musa Argentina

Celebre Tango Argentina

Espiga - Fortea

Tempo de Tango

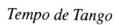

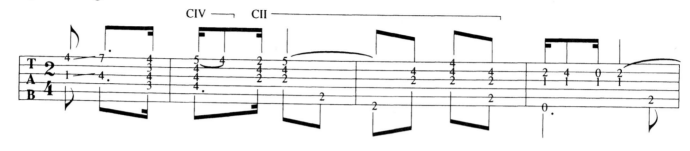

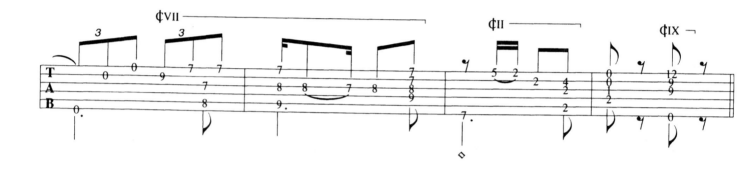

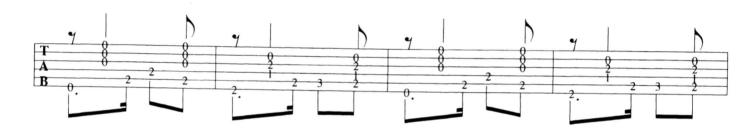

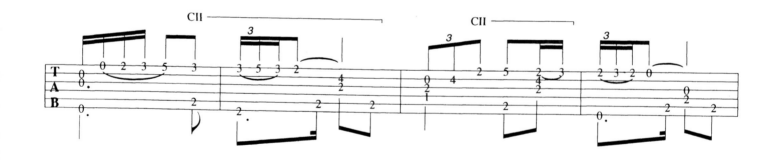

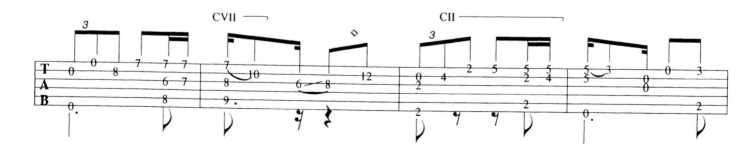

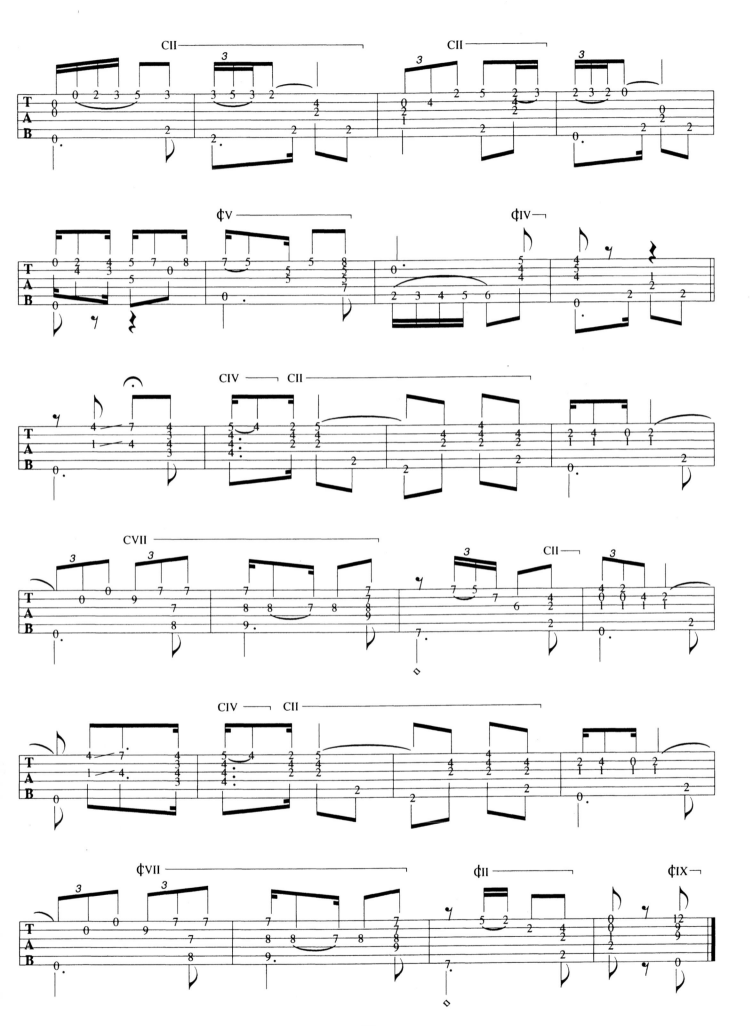

Tango

Francesco Tárrega

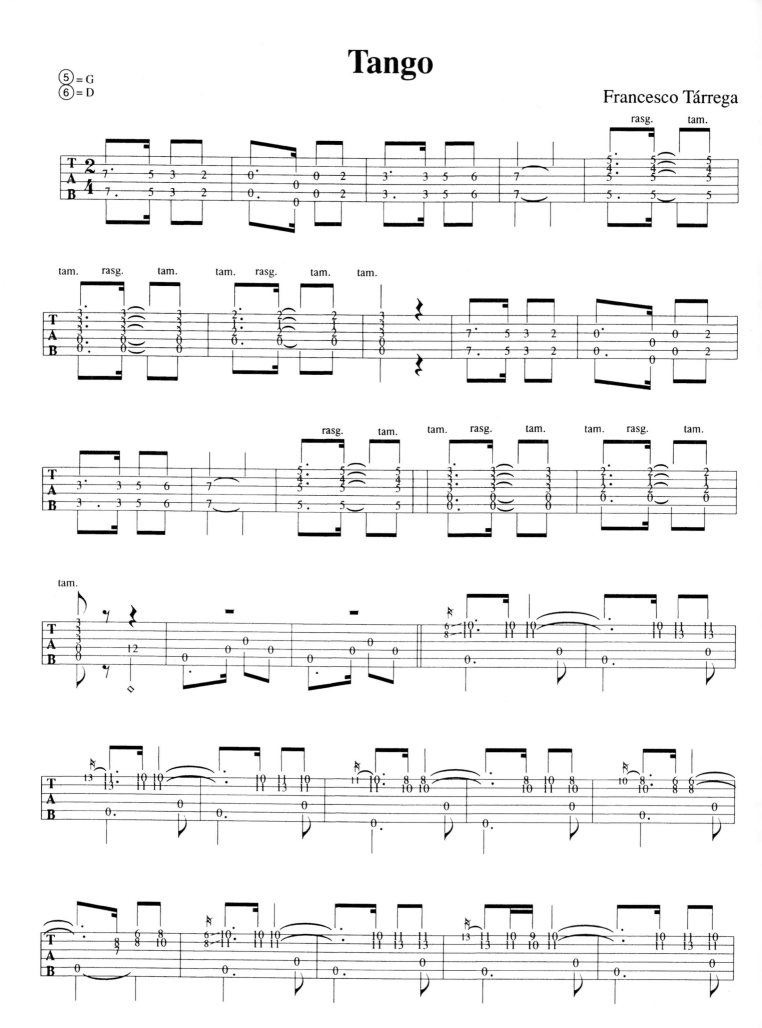

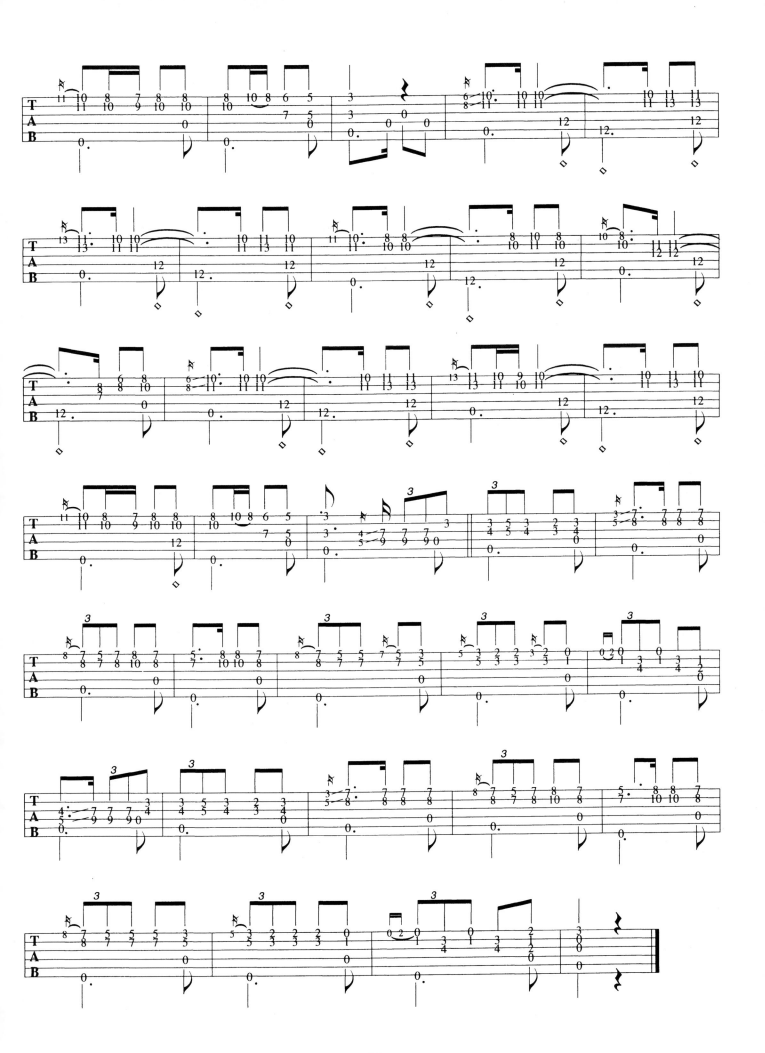

91

La Paloma

S. Yradier
F. Tárrega

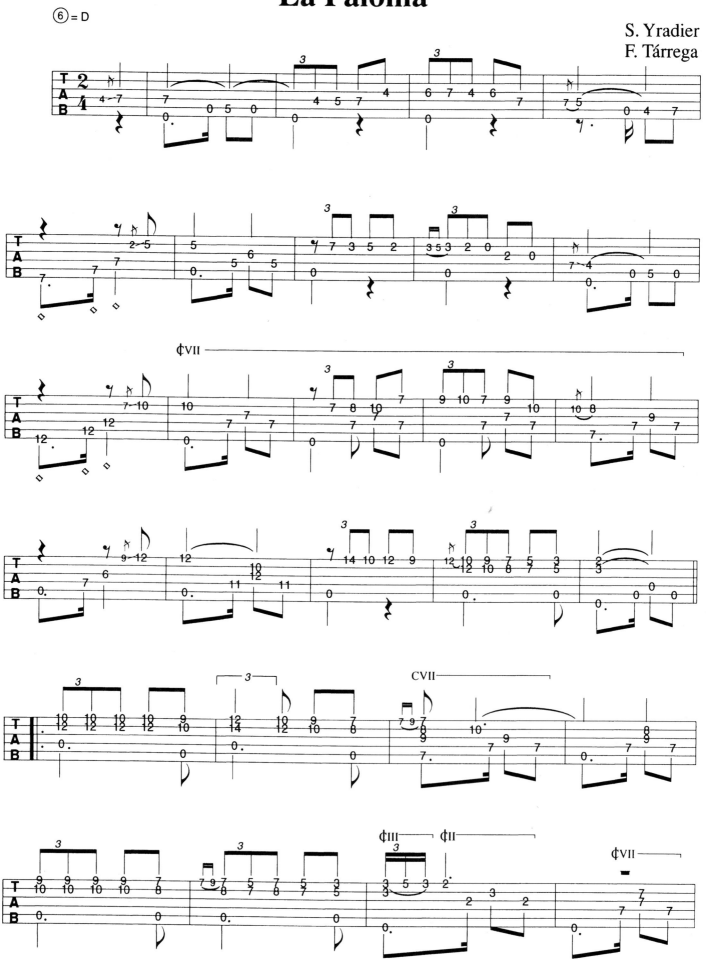

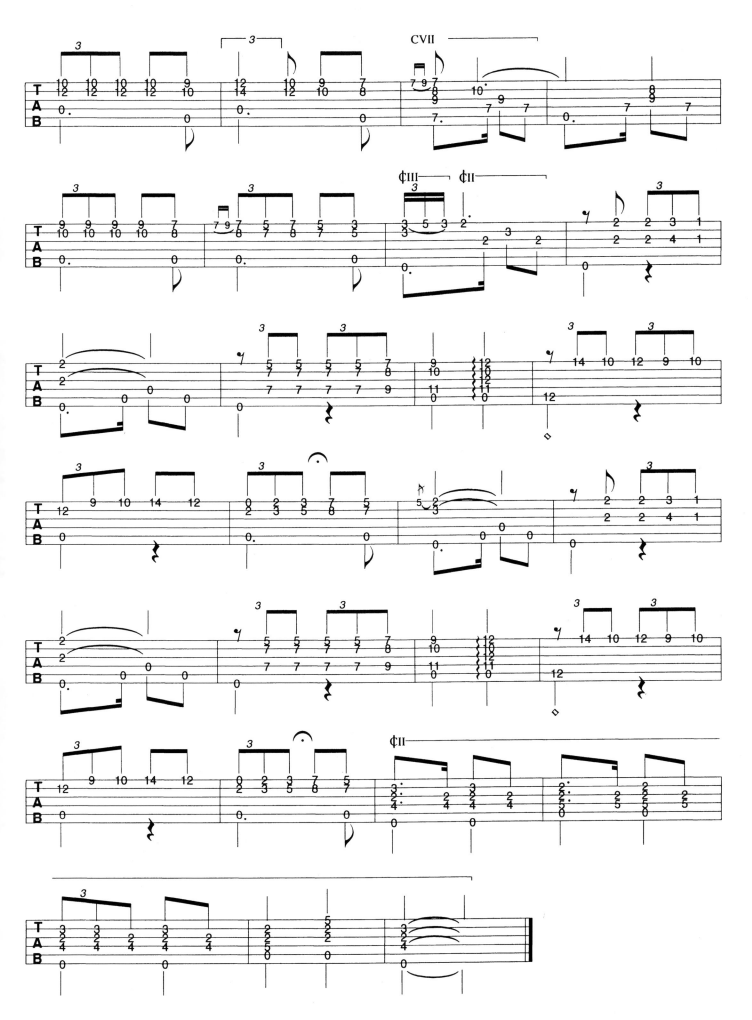

'O sole mio

Tango

E. di Capua
Transcription by F. Tárrega

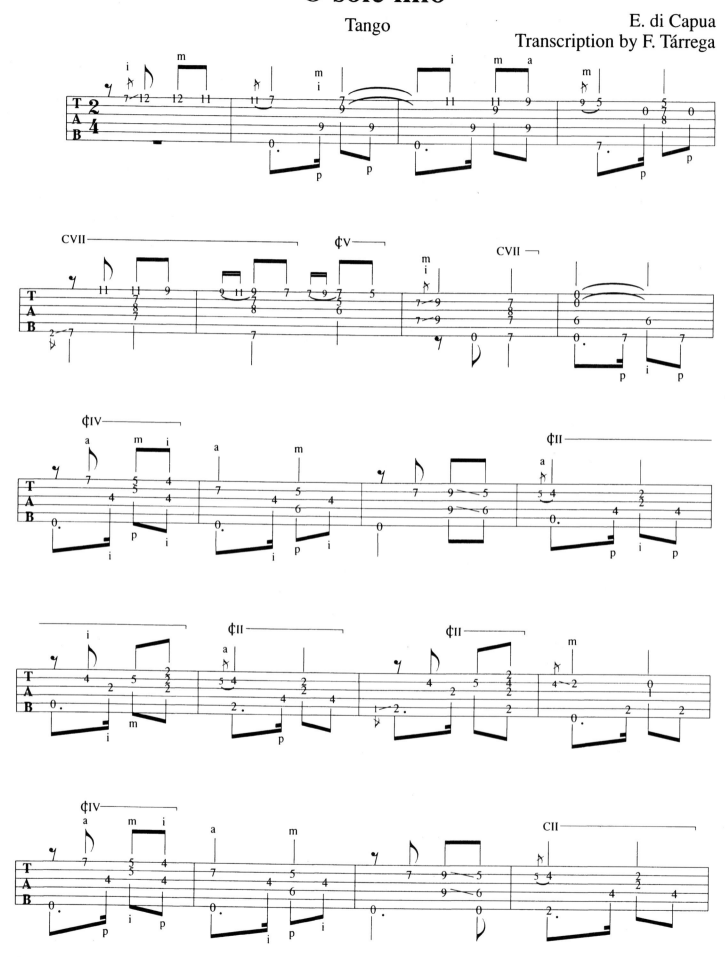

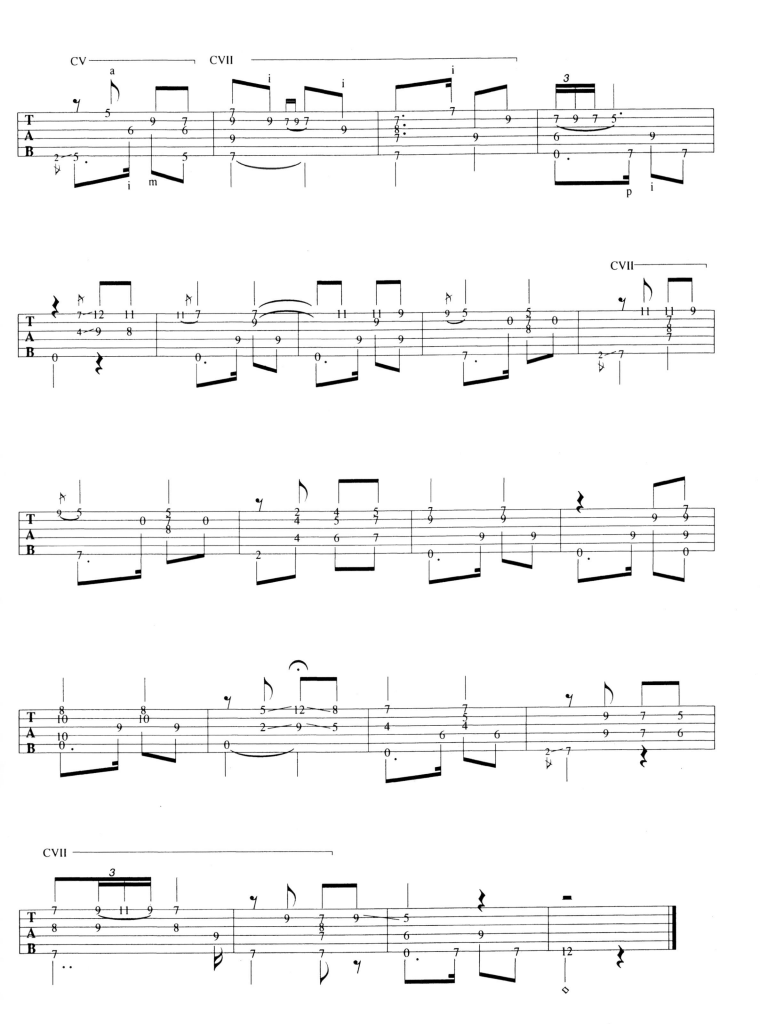

Del Ferrol a La Habana

Collection of Tangos for Guitar

J. Parga

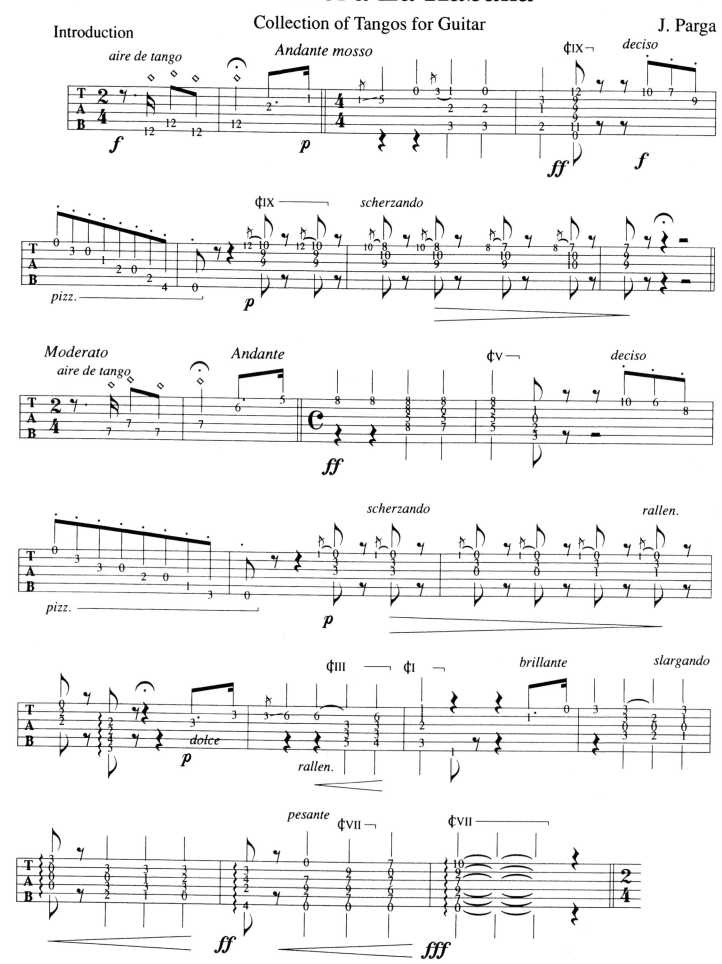

This page has been left blank
to avoid awkward page turns.

(Del Ferrol a La Habana)

No. 1

98

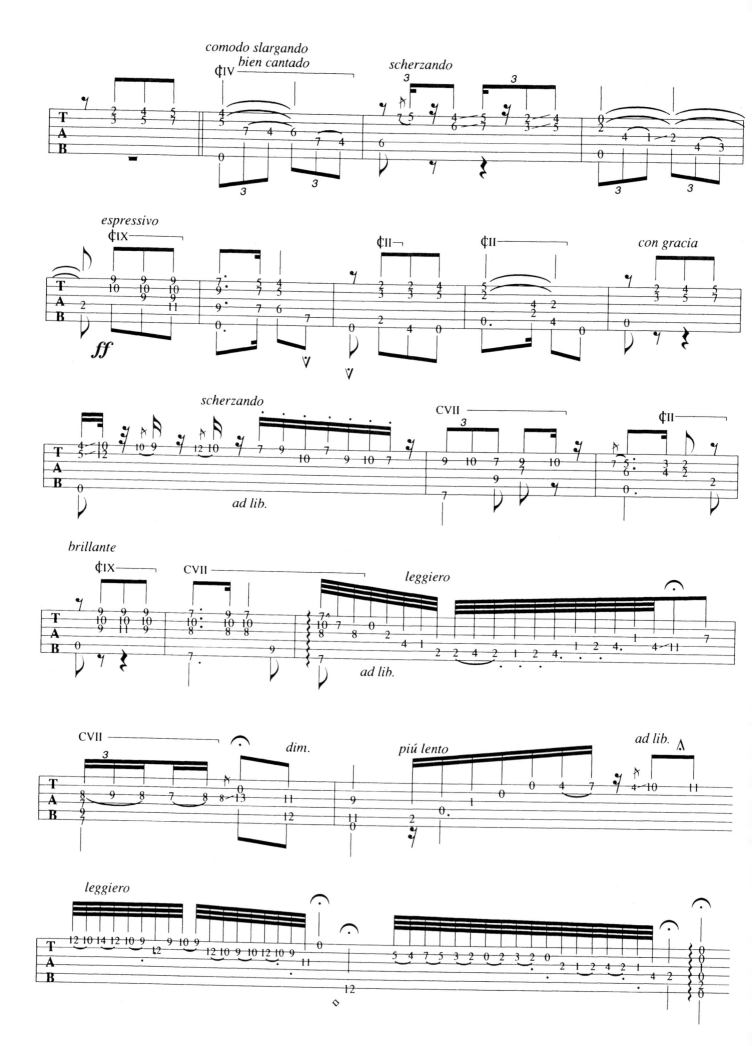

(proceed to No. 2)

(Del Ferrol a La Habana)

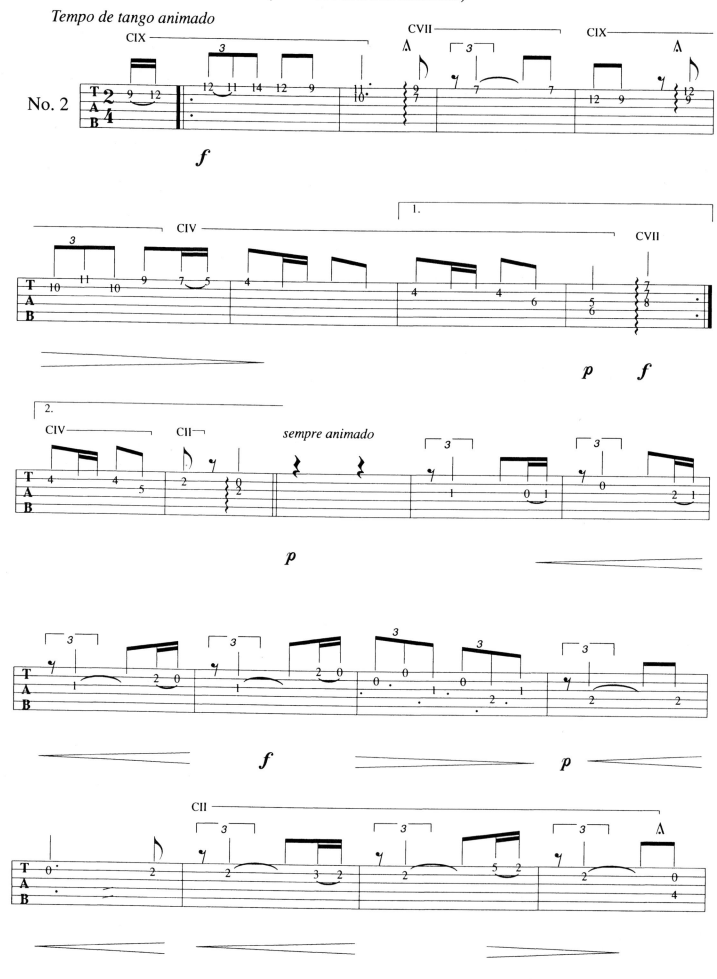

No. 2

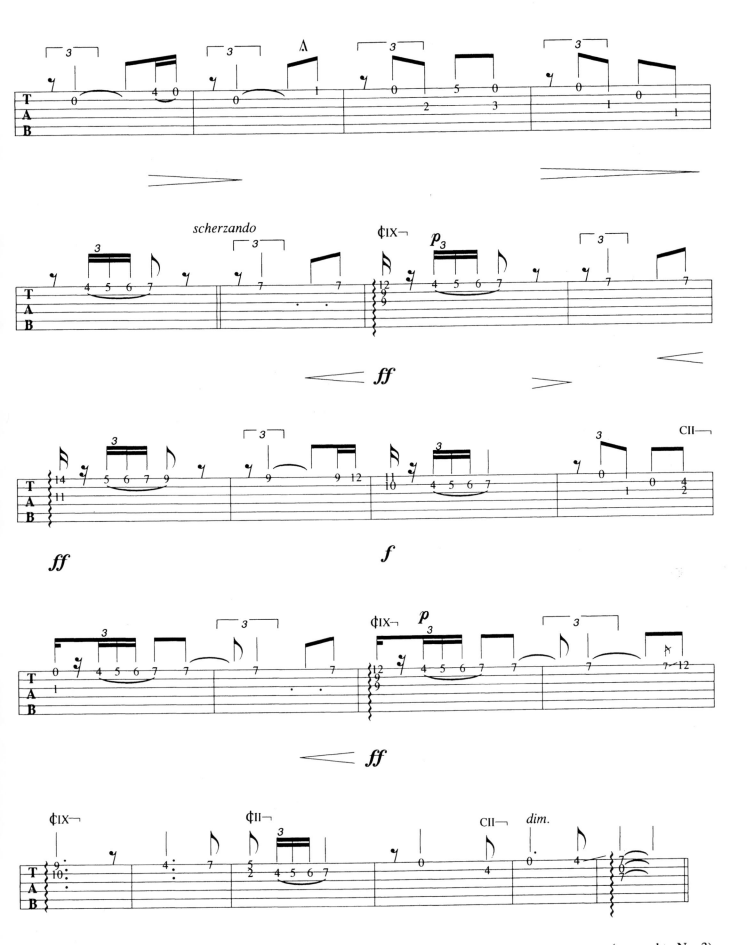

(proceed to No. 3)

(Del Ferrol a La Habana)

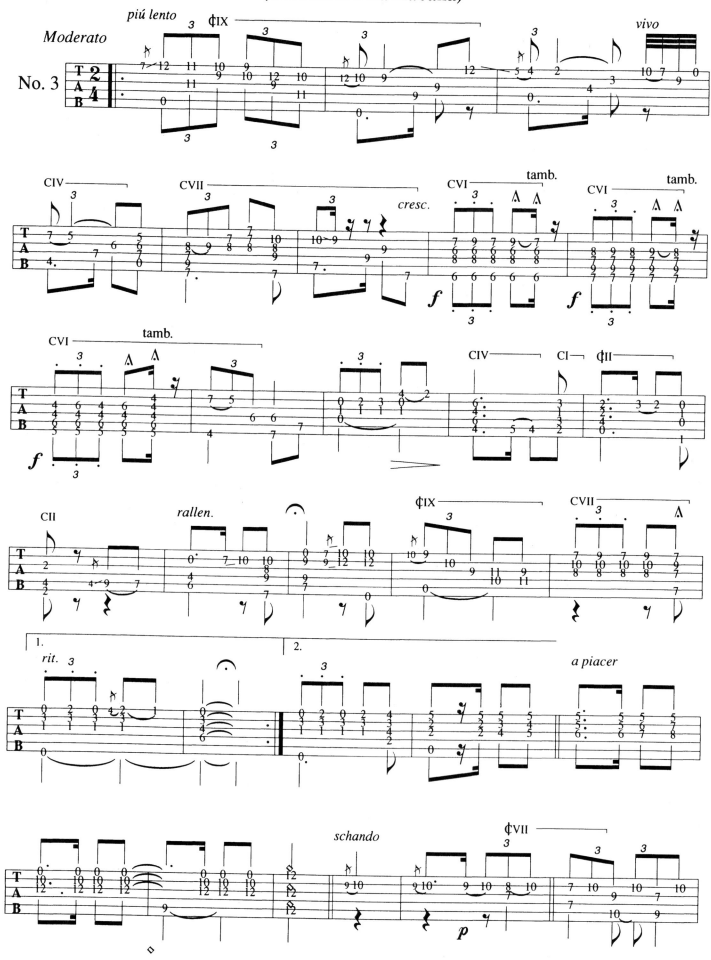

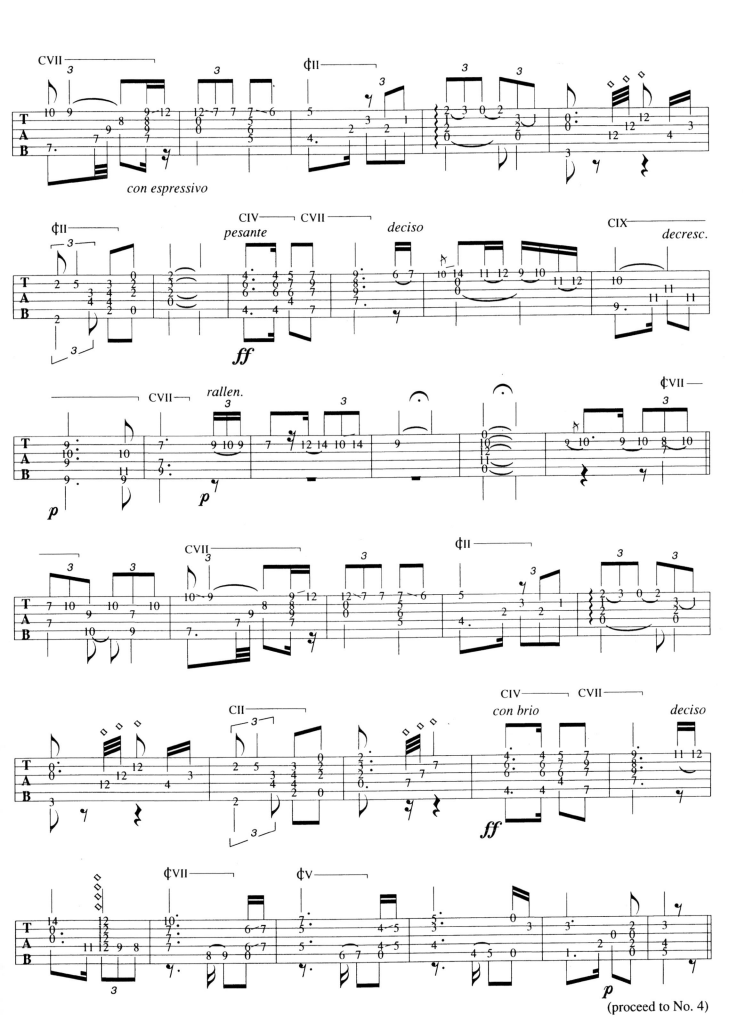

(Del Ferrol a La Habana)

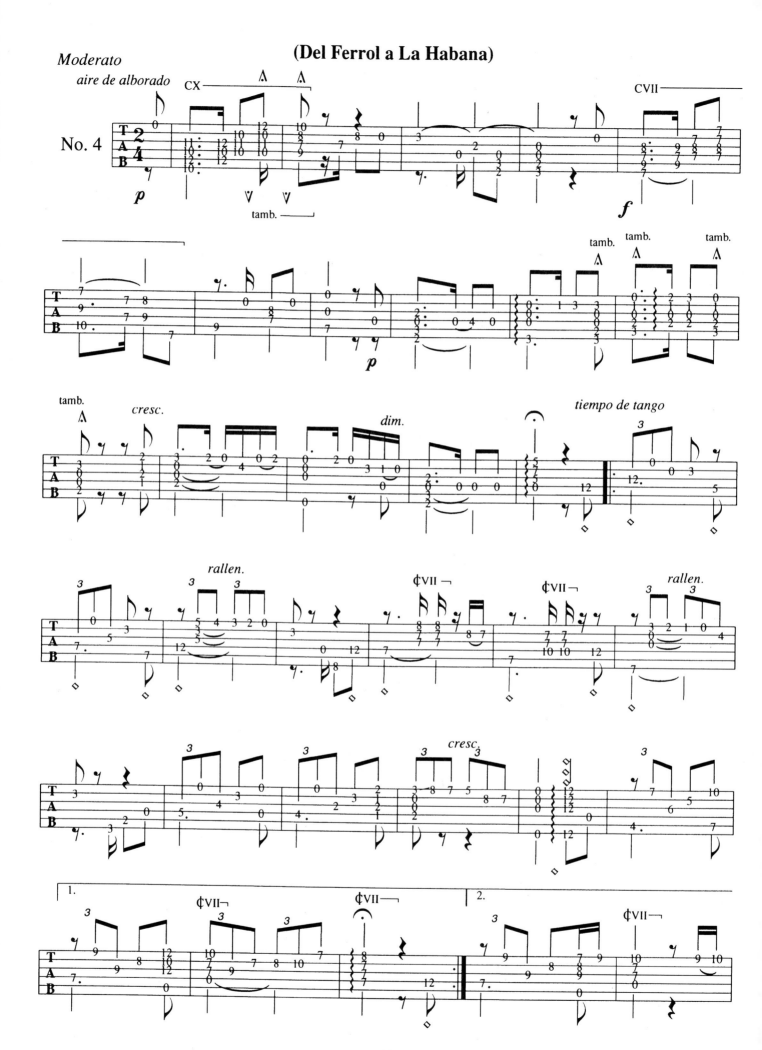

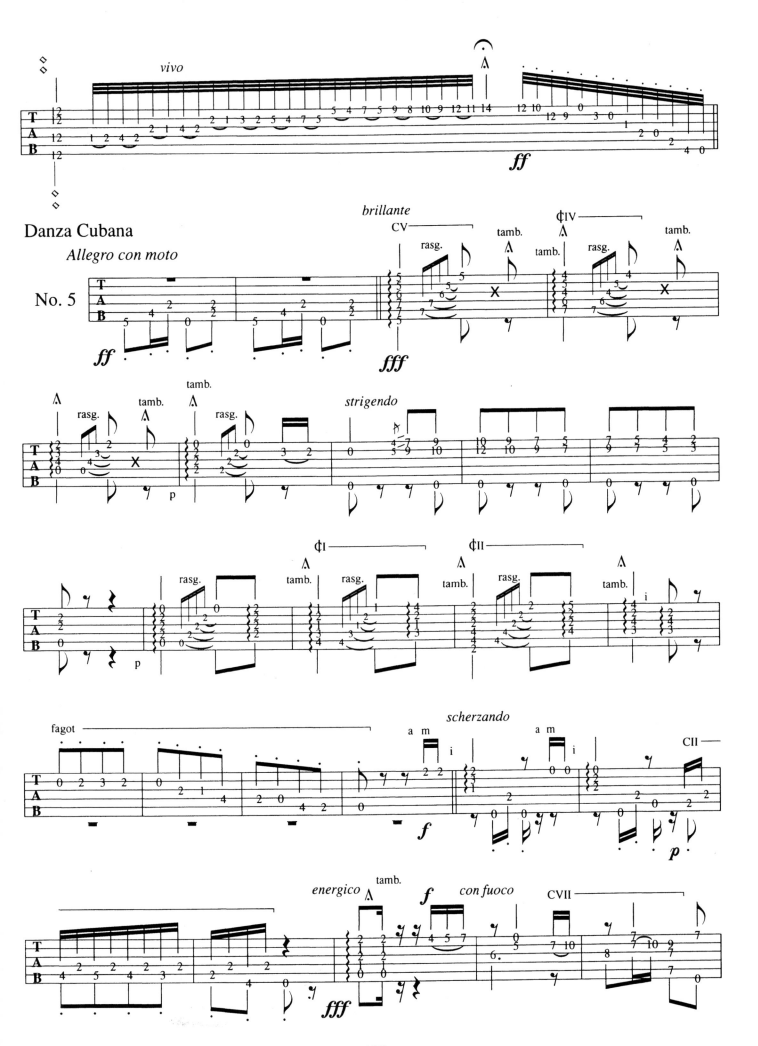

Danza Cubana

Allegro con moto

No. 5

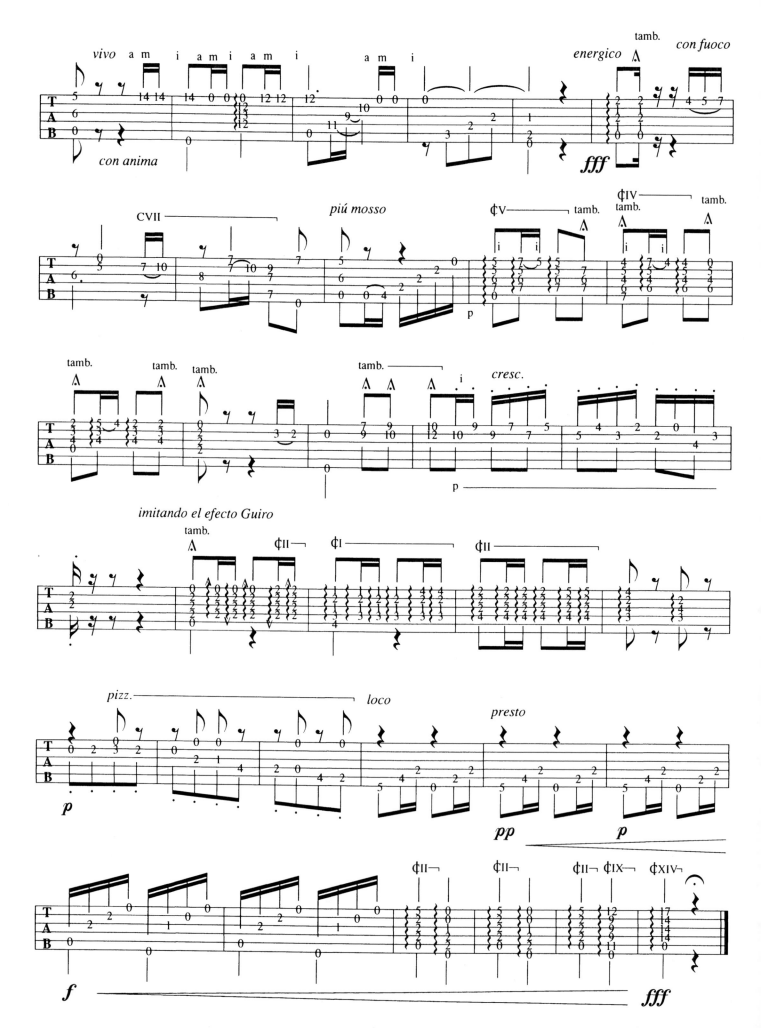

A ti solita!...

For Two Guitars   Habanera   F.P. Spreafico

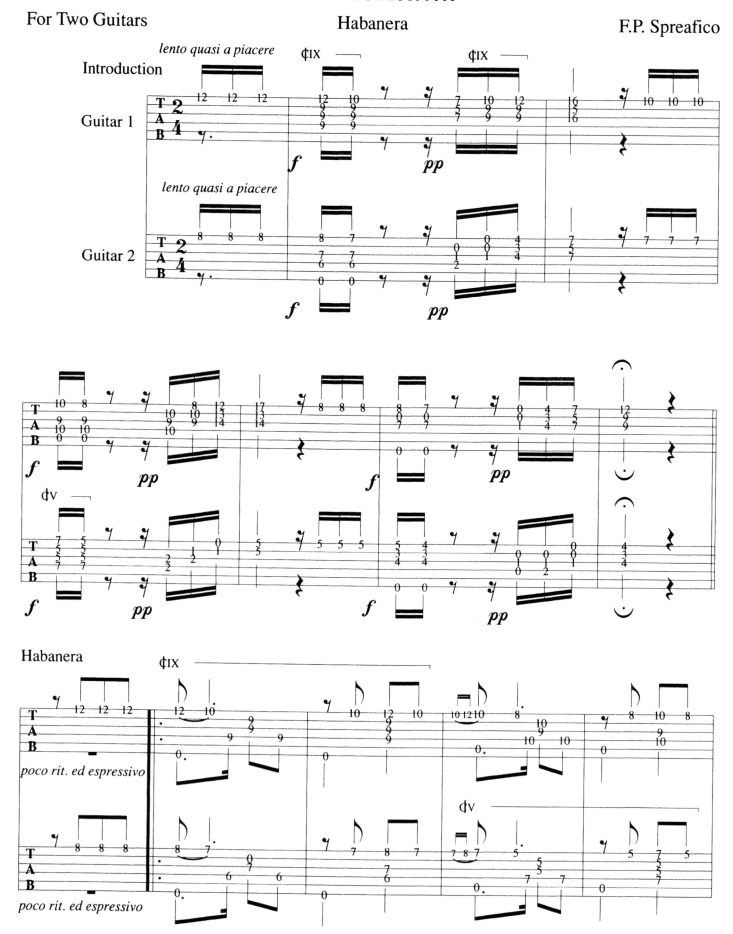

110

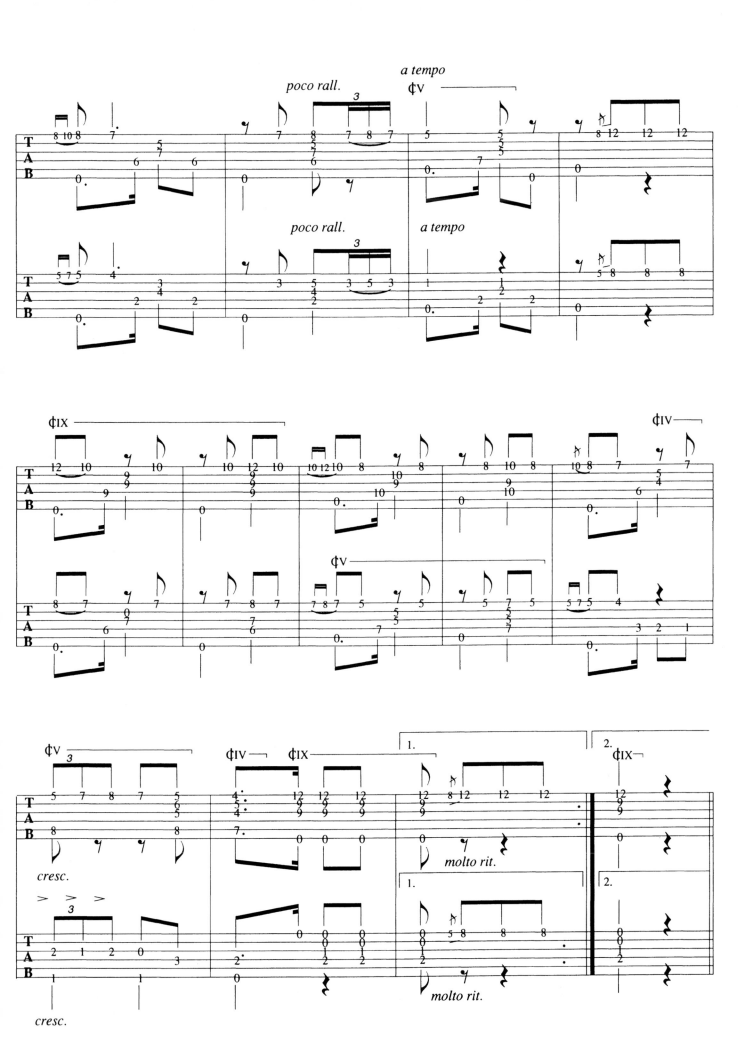

111

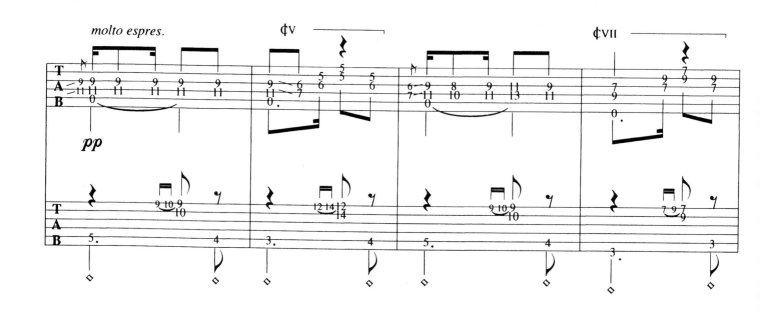

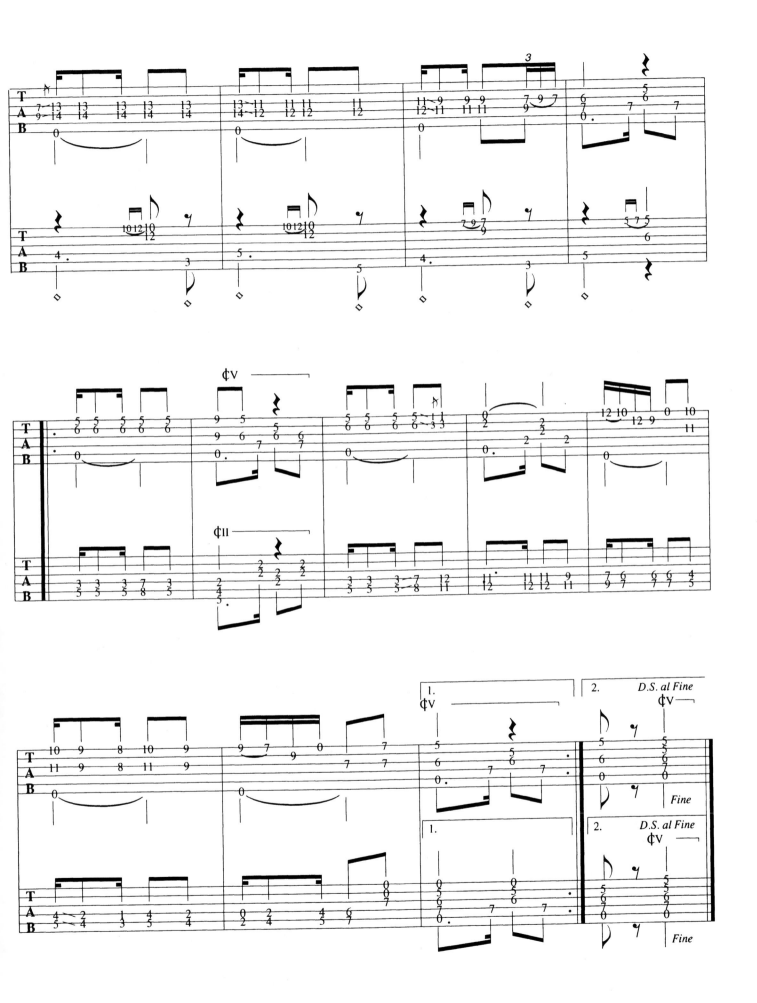

Clarita

Tango, Opus 3

Julian Ortiz

⑥ = D

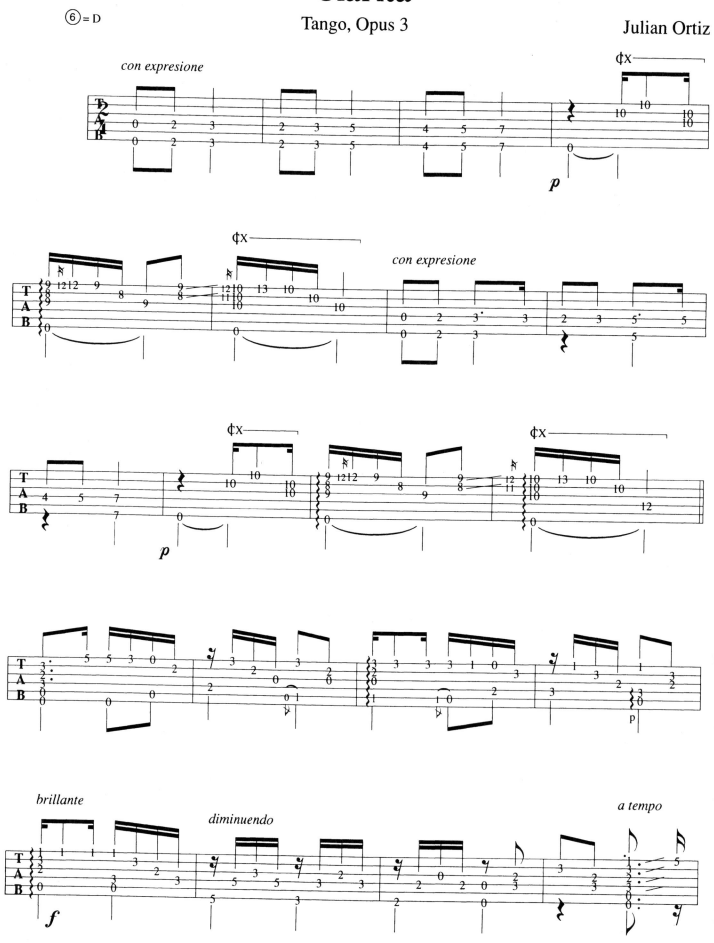

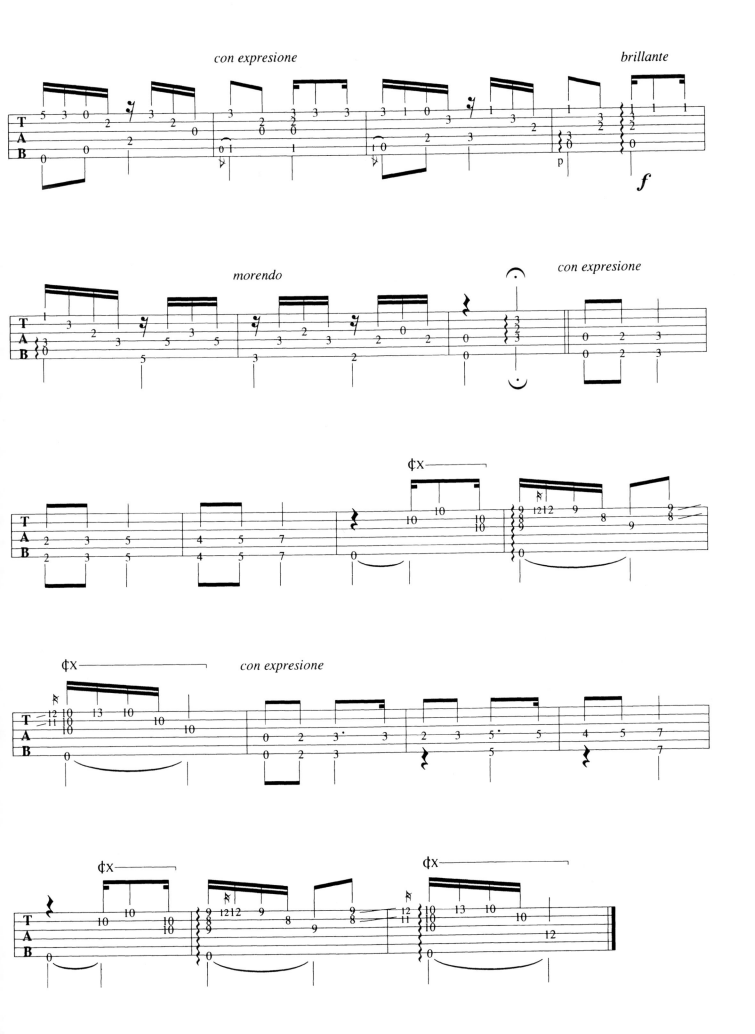

Anhelando

Tango de Salon

Julian Ortiz

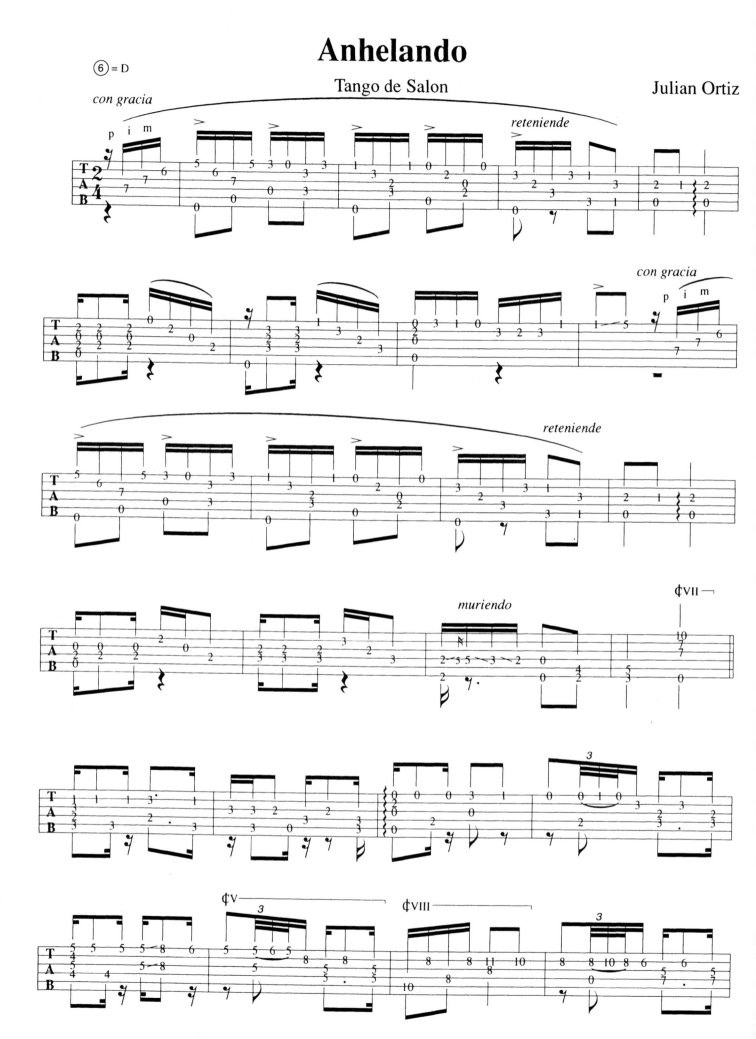

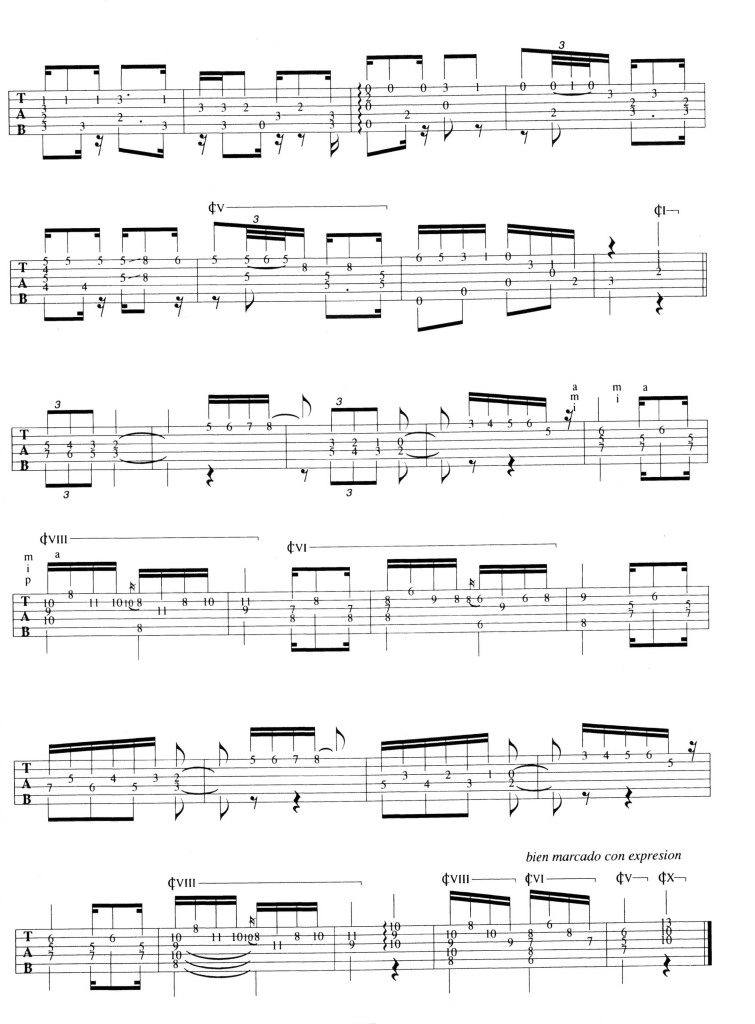

bien marcado con expresion

117

Junta al Farol

Tango Criollo

Vincente Caprino M.

This page has been left blank
to avoid awkward page turns.

Don Martín

Tango Criollo

Vincente Caprino M.

Fine

120

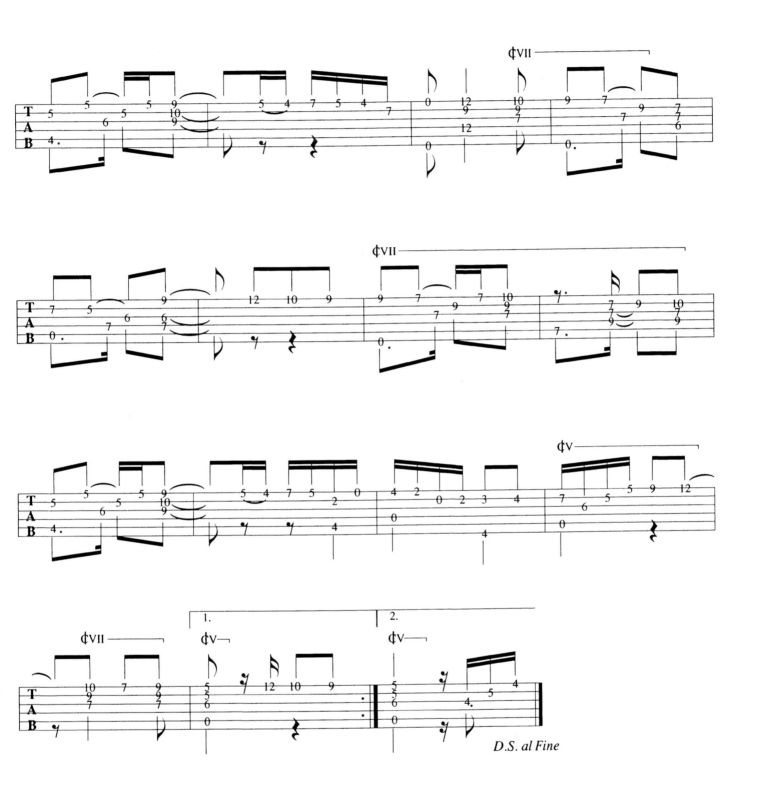

D. Juan Carlos

Tango Criollo

Vincente Caprino M.

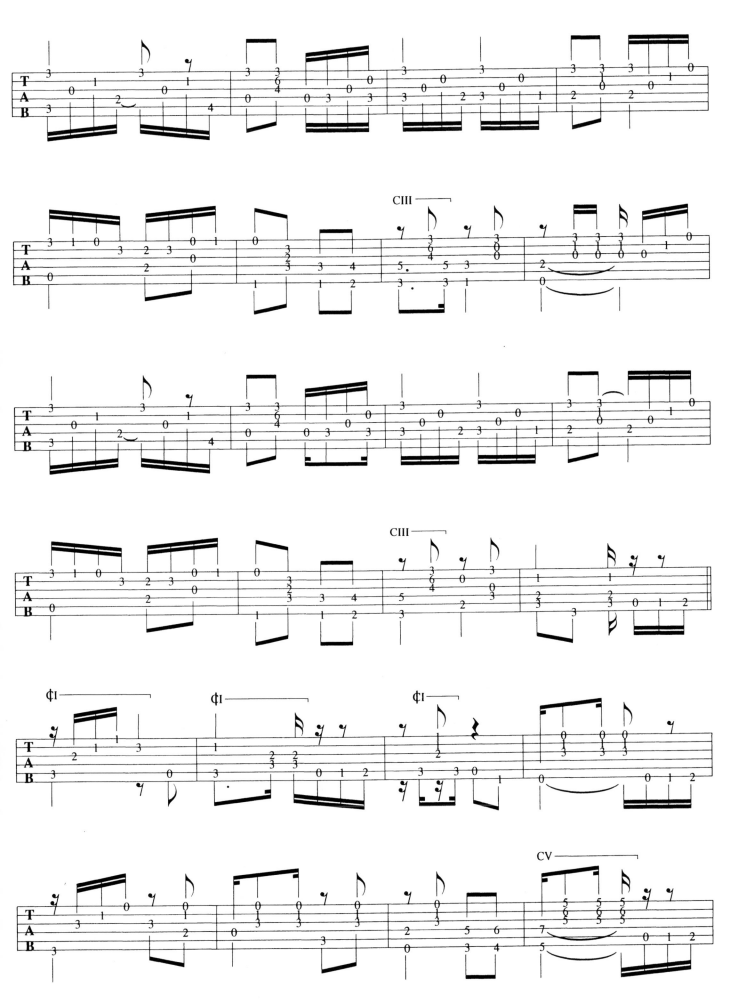

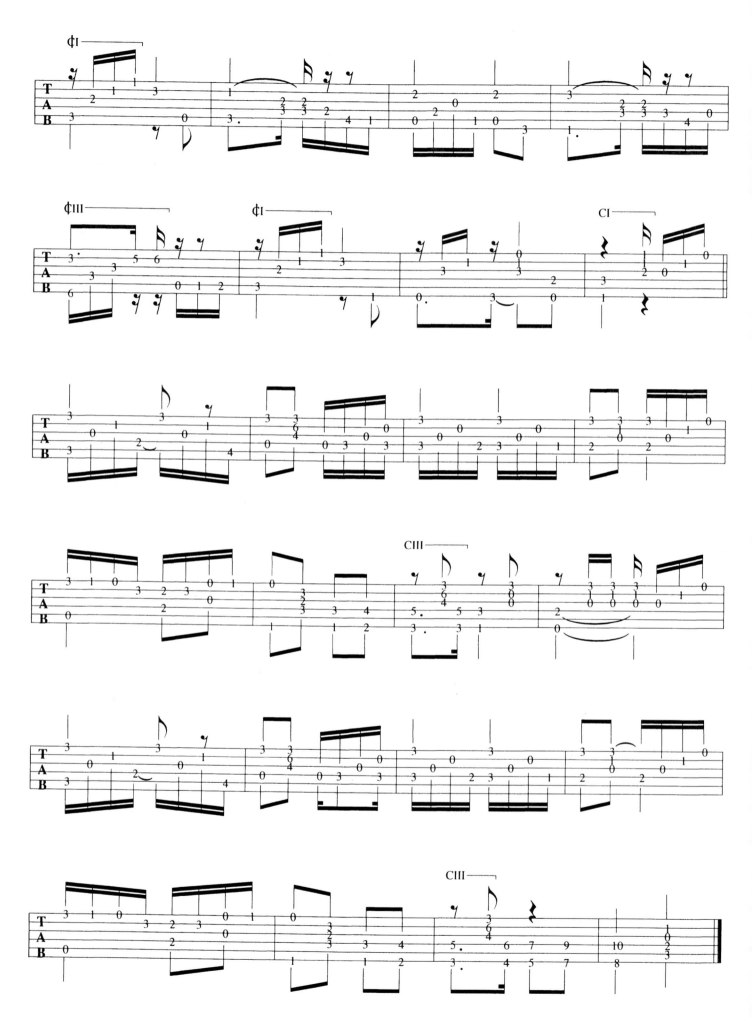

124

Romero

Tango

A. Galluzo

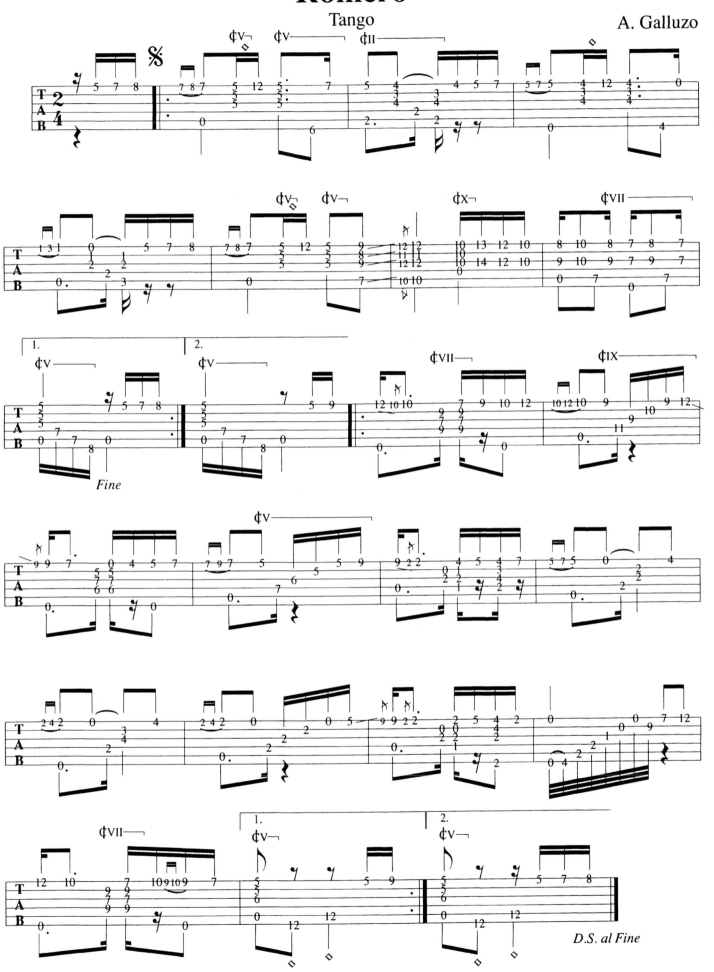

El Alero

Tango Pajuerano

Juan Maglio